# AYLA

# AYLA

## SANTOSH SHAH

A Feast of Nepali Dishes from Terai, Hills and the Himalayas

# A cuisine of geodiversity

**It is a dream come true to publish my first cookbook and to share the unique and beautiful flavours of Nepali food with the world. Until my time on BBC's UK *MasterChef: The Professionals*, few people knew what our cuisine was and I am really excited to be able to shine a light on one-of-a-kind ingredients and cooking techniques so that you can experience this cuisine for yourself at home. I spent several months in Nepal researching these amazing recipes, and I hope you will love them as much as I do.**

Why Ayla? Ayla has many meanings, but to me it means celebrations. It is technically a traditional Nepali spirit made from fermented sugarcane molasses with malt or grains and is served as a sagoon (love token) at joyous occasions. Each year we celebrate more than 50 festivals and our food culture is strongly based on these traditions, where growing and giving becomes one – the chapter on Festival Food is dedicated to this aspect of Nepali life. A good example is Yomari, a sweet, fish-shaped, steamed dumpling, filled with a molasses toffee and sesame seed paste (see page 136 for my take on this iconic recipe). It is prepared during the Yomari Punhi festival in December and is a product of the first harvested rice – warm, comforting and sustaining on a cold winter's day.

I also want to share with you my love for the land and its produce, and to celebrate the biodiversity that comes from it. For a country that only extends 885km (c550 miles) from west to east and 201km (c125 miles) from north to south, Nepal has a unique geographical structure. Three regions, three bands parallel to each other, define Nepal: the arid Himalayan high mountains, the middle hills – rich in green valleys, rivers and lakes – and the tropical grasslands of the Terai. In the high Himalayas, 3000m (c9840ft) and above, small farming communities still grow crops and raise livestock using the inherited knowledge of their ancestors who learned to deal with harsh weather conditions and high altitude. In the temperate climate of the high hills, 1800–2800m (c5900–9200ft), we grow cabbages, root vegetables and greens, while the sub-tropical middle hills, 1000–1800m (c3230–5900ft), have the perfect climate for citrus fruit, peaches, apples,

tomatoes and aubergines (eggplants). Further south, in the tropical Terai you will find mangoes, papayas, bananas, passion fruit, avocados, sugar cane and endless rice paddies. Although some rice crops are cultivated on the plateaux, three quarters of Nepal's rice production is in the Terai. The tropical and sub-tropical areas of Nepal rely on the summer monsoon to grow crops. But every year the start, length, and amount of rainfall during the monsoon is different and can have devastating effects on agriculture. This is one of the reasons why we rely on fermentation, to save the crops and extend our supplies throughout the long winters. Our most famous preserve, gundruk (see page 12), is made with green leaves, often from radish or mustard plants, fermented and dried. Gundruk will keep for many months and is used throughout the winter in soups, stews and pickles. Fermentation is not just a preservation process. It helps digestion and improves nutrition. Knowledge of what is good for you, and the use of herbs and spices to nurture the body is integrated into Nepali cooking and follows the Ayurvedic and Chinese medicinal traditions. I emphasise this on pages 12–17, by highlighting the health benefits of each ingredient.

My joy as a chef comes from playing with flavours and re-inventing traditional recipes without losing their essence. Take, for example, jimbu (see page 12), a wild garlic leaf that grows on the pastures of the Himalayan plateaux. It is mainly used as tempering, heated in hot oil, to drizzle over lentil stews. But jimbu can be used in many different ways; dehydrated and reduced to powder, it brings the flavour of a marinade to a whole new level and works particularly well with lamb.

Very little has been published on Nepali cuisine, yet Kathmandu hosts 48 culinary schools with an average of 600 students per school. I have lectured at these colleges and am proud to have inspired and encouraged a love of cooking in my students. I want this book to be a reference for them as well as a journey of discovery and inspiration for the home cook, through the Nepali provinces, from the far western states to its most eastern point, from its luscious lands and rivers to the arid high altitude crops. If my life has pulled me away from Nepal, my heart has never left.

# A personal map of Nepal

I have pinpointed on this map the places that define my Nepal: Mount Everest as a geological wonder, Lumbini as the start of Buddhism, Pashupatinath Temple, which is one of the most sacred in Hinduism, and my village in the heart of the Terai, where my journey started.

INDIA

CHINA

H i m a l a y a s

Api △
Byasrikh Himal
Saipal △
Asajatuppa △
Kanjiroba △
Dhaulagiri Himal
Annapurna Hima
Dhanlagiri △
Annapurna △

Jumla

Amargadhi
Manma

Bhimdatta

Dhangadhi

Tikapur

Jajarkot
Musikot

Baglung
Pokhara

Salyan

Sandhikharka
Sankhar

Kohalpur
Tulsipur

Nepalganj
Bhalubang
Butwal

Siddhartanaga

Lumbini ②

### 1. Mount Everest
Peaking at 8,849m (29,032ft), Mount Everest is the highest of the Himalayan mountains and the highest point on Earth. In Nepal, we call Everest Sagarmatha.

### 2. Lumbini – birthplace of Buddha
Prince Siddhartha Gautama, who later found enlightenment and became Lord Buddha, was born in the Lumbini gardens in 623 BCE. Today the Lumbini archaelogical remains and gardens are one of the four sacred pilgrimage sites for Buddhists.

### 3. Pashupatinath Temple
Located on the Bagmati river, on the eastern outskirts of Kathmandu, the Pashupatinath Temple, dedicated to Lord Shiva, is a masterpiece of Hindu architecture.

### 4. Karjanha – my birthplace
I grew up in Karjanha with my two sisters and five brothers. A small village, in the province of Siraha, 50km (31 miles) north-east of Janakpur, it is typical of the Terai: jade green rice paddies and colourful markets selling home-grown fruit and vegetables.

# Ingredients directory

Here you will find a brief description of some of the Nepali ingredients I use in my recipes. Most of them can be found in Asian food shops and supermarkets. As Nepali cuisine is starting to gain in popularity, many essential ingredients can now be ordered online on websites such as www.nepalfoodsonline.co.uk

## Bire noon (Himalayan black salt)

Black salt is a processed salt obtained from heating rock salt extracted from the hills close to the Himalayas with other compounds. The chemical transformation produces sulphur which gives black salt its "rotten egg" flavour. Its sodium content is lower than sea salt, and it is used as a spice for its umami flavour more than as a salt. It is used as a seasoning in the Chana Chatpate (see page 34).

**Recipes:** Crispy Potato & Puffed Rice Salad, page 34; Tamarind Chutney, page 159.

## Karkalo ko pat (colocasia *or* taro leaf)

Shaped like elephant ears, these are the leaves of the taro plant. Like the root, the raw leaves are toxic and should always be cooked. They contain a high concentration of calcium oxalate that can be irritating for the skin, mouth and throat. Washing and cooking the leaves thoroughly eliminates this problem. In Nepal, for the same reason, we sometimes wilt the leaves in the sun before cooking them.

Taro leaves can be found in Asian food shops, usually sold rolled and wrapped up. They acquire a sweet nutty flavour and a unique velvety texture when cooked. We use them steamed and in stir-fries, as you would other greens.

**Recipe:** Colocasia Leaves Curry, page 96.

## Gundruk (dried fermented greens)

Gundruk is a preparation of fermented and dried leafy greens. Mustard, radish, cauliflower or cabbage greens are harvested after the monsoon throughout the winter.

The leaves are wilted, fermented in large earthenware or plastic jars for a couple of weeks, then dried in the sun. Gundruk, which started as a necessity to cope with the monsoon months when vegetables are scarce, has become a way of life. Its addictive sourness enhances soups, salads and dals – see how to make it on page 21.

**Recipes:** Fermented Greens & Potato Soup, page 115; Fermented Greens & Soybean Salad, page 161.

## Hing (asafoetida)

Hing is the gummy resinous substance secreted by the root of *Ferula asafoetida,* a cousin of carrot and fennel. The top of a very large four-year old root is exposed to the air, incised and left in the ground while the resin slowly exudes from the plant. Over a period of three months, the resin is gradually collected, a fresh slice of root is exposed, and more incisions are made to allow more to ooze out. As it dries, the resin becomes hard and dark and develops its strong sulphurous smell, giving it its name which derives from Farsi (asa) and Latin (foetida): "stinking resin".

Hing can be bought crushed or powdered. It is the powdered hing that I use in the recipes in this book. When added to a hot oil, it loses its potency and becomes a spice close in flavour to shallots or garlic. In Nepal, we also use hing as a herbal remedy to help with asthma, epilepsy and digestion.

**Recipes:** Sherpa Noodle Soup, page 71; Black Dal, page 94; Himalayan Yam Curry, page 98; Plantain Curry, page 101; Sour Yogurt Soup, page 117; Meat Garam Masala, page 193; Vegetable Garam Masala, page 194.

## Jimbu (Himalayan leaf garlic)

Jimbu is part of the allium family and grows wild in the Himalayan central high hills. It is harvested from June to September, and then dried to be used during the winter months. It is sold in markets all over Nepal. Jimbu is also used as a remedy against cough and stomach pain. The flavour is a mix of garlic, chives and shallot. A good substitute is the green part of a spring onion (scallion), but I sometimes use garlic cloves. Fresh jimbu is not readily available outside of Nepal, but you can buy dried jimbu from Nepali food shops and online. Its flavour is brought back to life when used in tempering (see page 20).

**Recipes:** Spiced Chicken Salad, page 36; Glazed Stir-fried Wild Boar Belly, page 59; Black Dal, page 94.

## Jhhau (stone moss)

I use stone moss in some of my garam masala spice mix preparations. It is dried lichen with a woody flavour which acts as a taste enhancer. You can find it online or it can be specially ordered from Nepali food shops.

**Recipes:** Nepali Garam Masala, page 190; Meat Garam Masala, page 193.

## Jwanu *or* ajwain (carom seeds)

Technically, they are not seeds but fruits, like cumin, coriander (cilantro) and fennel, all part of the Apiaceae family. Their flavour is similar to dried thyme, only slightly more bitter.

In Nepal, carom seeds are sometimes chewed raw to help digestion, or infused like tea for stomach troubles because of their anti-bacterial properties.

They are one of the main flavours in the Quawati (see page 131), the restorative sprouted bean soup served during the Janai Purnima festival. Nepali people are fond of jwanu and also often mix them into a bread dough before baking.

**Recipes:** Spiced Spinach, Fig & Potato Croquettes, page 30; Crispy Onion Beignets, page 39; Fried Breaded Prawns (shrimp), page 83; Pointed Gourd Tempura, page 108; Sprouted Bean Soup, page 131.

## Karela (bitter gourd)

Easy to find in any Asian market, kerala is a bright green, elongated gourd, with a rough, knobbly texture. Part of the gourd family, karela is also named bitter gourd because of its intensely bitter flavour, which for some is an acquired taste. High in fibre, vitamins and minerals, it is praised in Ayurvedic medicine for lowering blood pressure and sometimes used as an insulin alternative for treating diabetes.

Inside the rugged shell is a spongy centre with seeds. The interior is white when unripe, turning red when the kerala ripens. The seeds and flesh are removed and only the shell is used in cooking.

**Recipes:** Stuffed Bitter Gourd, page 112; Bitter Gourd Chutney, page 147.

## Lapsi (Nepali hog plum)

Lapsi looks like a small plum, with a skin colour ranging from green to yellow. Also known as Nepali hog plum, it is part of the Anacardiaceae family which includes over 700 varieties of species, amongst them: cashews, mangoes and sumac. Lapsi trees are spread all over Asia and are abundant in the Himalayan hills. September to January is harvesting time and most of the production is preserved in chutneys and reserved to make an extremely popular sweet and sour candy called titaura. The sourness of lapsi stimulates the production of gastric juices and when consumed in moderation, helps digestion.

Unfortunately, as of now, they are not exported. I have included lapsi in several recipes and suggested tamarind pulp (see method for making on page 17) as a substitute. If, however you can get hold of them, here is a simple method to extract the pulp: boil the lapsi in water until they are very soft, leave to cool, then crush the fruit between your fingers to remove the stones (pits) and pass the whole mixture through a fine sieve (strainer).

**Recipes:** Goat Curry with Lapsi Berries, page 55; Glazed Stir-fried Wild Boar Belly, page 59.

## Tori (mustard seeds & mustard oil)

In Nepal, we widely use the produce of the mustard plant. The leaves are cooked or fermented and dried; the seeds are used to make pickles, flavour curries or are pressed to extract mustard oil. Because of their antibacterial properties, mustard seeds are the perfect ingredient for making pickles and chutneys. They range from a dark brown to a pale yellow, the dark being more pungent. Mustard seeds are often combined with fish to balance flavour.

You need a 3–3.5kg (6–6¾lb) mix of white and dark mustard seeds to produce 1 litre (4 cups) of mustard oil. Unfortunately, the artisan mustard oil mills are disappearing in Nepal. A lot of other oils have taken over the market, including blended mustard oils. But for many, including myself, pure mustard oil is part of the authentic flavour of Nepali cuisine. Like ghee (clarified butter), it also has the advantage of withstanding very high temperatures.

Mustard oil is also used as a sinus remedy and a massage oil to help inflammation and pain.

Mustard oil is used in many recipes throughout the book, but it plays a more prominent role in the recipes listed here.

**Recipes:** White Fish in Mustard & Onion Sauce, page 80; Spiced Chargrilled Jackfruit, page 107; Yellow Mustard Paste, page 197.

## Neguro (fiddlehead fern)

These are the young curled up leaves of edible ferns. They are one of the most popular wild vegetables in Nepal, foraged in the spring, along rivers, damp fields and in the mountains. We eat the tightly curled up leaves as well as the unfolded young fronds.

Not every fern frond is edible. If you are foraging fiddlehead ferns, look for bright green shoots, with u-shaped stems and a brown, paper-like skin attached to its top. Any frond covered with a whitish fuzz is poisonous and should not be picked.

Before cooking neguro, remove any trace of brown skin and wash well under running water. They are fragile and should be cooked soon after harvesting. They can also be blanched then frozen.

**Recipe:** Fiddlehead Fern Curry, page 105.

## Parwal (pointed gourd)

Parwal is a vine-grown vegetable that belongs to the cucumber and gourd family. Small, oblong and yellowish-green with light stripes, you will easily spot it in Asian food shops. Rich in vitamins, parwal is a healthy vegetable used in Ayurvedic medicine as a digestive stimulant and liver protector.

Like any gourd, parwal has an absorbent flesh perfect for marinades and its skin remains crunchy when deep-fried.

To prepare, just scrape the skin with a hard brush or the back of a knife to remove any bumps. Take out the larger seeds, keeping the small, slightly slimy seedy centre intact.

**Recipe:** Pointed Gourd Tempura, page 108.

## Bhat (plain rice), bhuja (puffed rice) and chiura (beaten rice)

Rice is our most important crop in Nepal. Three quarters of the production is cultivated in the Terai, the rest on the hills and high plateaux of the Himalayas. The National Paddy Day which takes place at the end of June or beginning of July is dedicated to the planting of rice. A day of singing and dancing where throwing yourself in the muddy rice fields is entirely part of the fun. The Newari people celebrate Yomari Punhi, a festival for the harvesting of rice, at the end of December (see page 121).

At home, we mainly eat Bhat (Plain Rice, see page 169) and reserve pulao rice dishes for celebrations.

Puffed rice is called bhuja and is commercially made by dry heating rice over an extremely high temperature, stirring constantly, until puffed up. The process only takes a few seconds. Bhuja is served as an accompaniment to street food and is the main ingredient in Chana Chatpate (Crispy Potato & Puffed Rice Salad, see page 34). In these recipes, you can use store-bought puffed rice for convenience.

Beaten rice, or chiura, was traditionally made by steaming, roasting, then beating the rice in a giant mortar with a pestle.

Today, the rice is roasted and compressed mechanically, and the grain separates into flat slices, similar to jumbo oats. The beaten rice flakes can then be toasted to add more flavour and are served alongside saucy curries, such as the Pork & Bamboo Shoot Curry on page 56.

## Sisnu (nettles)

Nettles are foraged in Nepal in the same way they are in Europe and North America. Rich in vitamins and minerals, they are the perfect ingredient for a restorative winter soup or a curry. To handle nettles, use rubber gloves or tongs. The stem and leaves are covered with tiny spines that sting and release formic acid which greatly irritates the skin. Once cooked, crushed, fermented or even frozen, there is no risk of irritation. The best nettle leaves for cooking are the young shoots at the top of the plant. They are at their best in the spring or early autumn (fall). Older leaves have less flavour. To keep their bright green colour, plunge the blanched leaves into iced water. The contrast between hot and icy-cold fixes the chlorophyl in the leaves.

**Recipe:** Potatoes with Nettles & Spinach, page 110.

## Sukeko kubhindo (sundried ash gourd)

This is a greenish-grey pumpkin, oblong or round, which takes its name from the aspect of its skin – a chalky coating that looks like white ash. The juice of the young ash gourd is known for its positive pranic properties. In Ayurveda, prana is your vital energy and positive pranic food will increase and balance that energy. Ash gourds are often grown in front of houses to radiate that positive energy. Ash gourd are thinly sliced and dried in the sun to be used in curries and soups all year round. I have not used this ingredient in the recipes featured in this book, but wanted to include it here, as it plays an important role in our Nepali cuisine.

## Tama (fermented bamboo shoots)

Tama is the name specifically used for fermented bamboo shoots. Bamboo shoots are the young shoots of the bamboo plant, sprouting from the ground, and picked before they reach 30cm (12in). The woody outer layers are peeled off to reveal a tender, ivory conical root. The young shoots of the bamboo plants are harvested from July to September, then peeled, sliced and boiled to remove any acrid taste and toxins. They are then covered with water, sometimes flavoured with turmeric, and left to ferment for about 10 days.

Tama are a good source of probiotics and rich in antioxidants. They are recommended to regulate blood pressure and prevent cardiovascular disease.

In Nepal, we like the sourness of tama and we use it widely in cooking. In fact, it is one of the ingredients you will surely find in Nepali shops around the world. Simply rinse the shoots under water, dry them, and they are ready to use.

**Recipes:** Pork & Bamboo Shoot Curry, page 56; Bamboo Shoot Pickle, page 152.

## Titiri (tamarind)

The tamarind is a large fruit tree that can reach 30m (almost 100ft) in height. It produces cinnamon-coloured oblong pods which contain a dark compact mixture of paste and seeds. Its sourness comes from a high content of tartaric acid. Tamarind trees are widely cultivated in the Terai.

Nepali people have an acquired taste for tang and sourness. Like lapsi (Nepali hog plum, see page 13), and citrus juices, tamarind is added to curries and made into chutneys to enhance flavour. Tamarind pulp makes a good substitute for lapsi pulp in the recipes in this book.

You can buy tamarind paste from supermarkets and Asian food shops, but it is often mixed with sugar, salt and citric acid, and sometimes preservatives. It is always best to buy the pure tamarind pulp sold as compressed blocks of pulp and seeds found in Asian food shops.

To make about 150ml ($\frac{2}{3}$ cup) of tamarind paste, place 80g (2¾oz) of compressed tamarind pulp and seeds in a bowl and cover with 200ml (¾ cup) of boiling water. Leave for 15 minutes, then work the pulp with your fingers to separate the seeds. Pass through a sieve (strainer),

pressing and rubbing the mixture with your fingers to extract as much paste as possible. The paste will keep in an airtight container in the refrigerator for 2–3 months. The compacted pulp, stored in an air-tight container, will last for at least 6 months.

## Tejpaat (Nepali bay leaves)

The bay leaves I use in my recipes are called tejpaat and are native to Nepal and northern India. Tejpaat is related to cinnamon and cassia. Tejpaat leaves are longer and wider than other bay leaves, with three distinctive veins running down their length. Its aroma is a subtle mix of cinnamon and clove. When freshly picked, the leaves are bright green. Dried, they turn greyish-green with a more muted flavour.

Often used as a tea remedy for coughs and asthma, the leaves have good anti-bacterial, anti-fungal properties and are known to help with digestion.

Tejpaat leaves are crucial to tempering (see page 20) and Garam Masala Spice Mixes (see pages 190–194). Crushed and stirred into hot oil or ghee (clarified butter), they come to life. They are widely available in Nepali and Asian food shops but if you cannot get hold of them just leave them out.

**Recipes:** Goat Curry with Lapsi Berries, page 55; Pork & Bamboo Shoot Curry, page 56; Glazed Stir-fried Wild Boar Belly, page 59; Red Junglefowl Curry, page 64.

## Timmur (Nepali Sichuan peppercorn)

Timmur is native to Nepal and is a cousin of the Sichuan peppercorn. It grows wild on prickly bushes, along the hills of the Himalayas, at 2000m (6500ft) altitude. Close in flavour, both peppercorns have a similar tingling effect on the tongue and palate, but timmur has an added lingering flavour of citrus and grapefruit.

The timmur berrries are picked in September and dried in the sun for a week. Only the husks are kept, the hard central seeds are discarded. It is often used in pickles and chutneys or to flavour dal. We export it for the perfume industry and as a trendy aromatic for gin. At home, it is our remedy for the common cold, cough, headaches and toothaches.

**Recipes:** Grilled Marinated Kebabs, page 41; Crispy Chilli Chicken, page 66; Sherpa Noodle Soup, page 71; Sesame & Green Chilli Pickle, page 150; Tomato Sesame Chutney, page 151; Timmur Spice Mix, page 189; Chatpate Spice Mix, page 189; Garam Masala Spice Mixes, pages 190–194.

## Tulsi (holy basil leaves)

We venerate the Tulsi plant for both therapeutic and religious reasons. It is considered as the queen of herbs in Ayurvedic medicine, a remedy for physical and psychological stress. In Hinduism, it is the terrestrial representation of the Goddess Tulsi, devoted to Lord Vishnu. The Chaturmas is a four-month period of atonement and fasting which starts at the end of July, during which Lord Vishnu rests, having provided us with a bounty of produce. On the day of Harishayani Ekadashi, which starts the Charturmas, Tulsi plants, which grow wild in Nepal, are symbolically planted around houses.

Holy basil tastes like clove with a peppery after taste. It should not be confused with Thai basil. You can buy Tulsi plants online.

**Recipe:** Masala Tea, page 209.

# Chef's tips and techniques

## COOKING TECHNIQUES

### Tempering (jhaneko)

Tempering means adding whole spices to a hot oil or ghee (clarified butter). The hot oil releases and retains the essential oils and flavours contained in the spices. Therefore, in addition to flavour, you get the full nutritional value of a spice carried into the dish.

Tempering is done either at the beginning, or towards the end of cooking, depending on the recipe. When done at the beginning, it allows the ingredients added after to better absorb the aroma and goodness of the spices. When done at the end, it adds an additional layer to the taste.

Timing is important in tempering. Make sure you have all your spices at hand before you start. The oil must be hot so always heat it first. A shimmer at the surface is usually a good indication of the perfect heat. The spices are added according to their cooking time to avoid any risk of burning. If they burn, it is best to start over or your dish will have an unpleasant acrid aftertaste. When the spices start crackling or popping it means the tempering is done. Each of my recipes that feature tempering will guide you through the stages and what to add next.

### Marination (moleko)

Marination has several purposes: it tenderizes, flavours and protects. Different ingredients can be used to obtain the desired effect.

Salt in a marinade will first draw moisture out of the meat and vegetables, then in a second stage, the meat or vegetable will soak back the moisture accumulated on the surface, drawing in the spices and flavours that were added. But eventually you will lose all the moisture so marinating with salt should be a short process.

Acid, like vinegar or citrus juice, has a similar effect to salt. It will break the protein and connective tissue at the surface of the meat and allow flavour to go through. But too much

acidity or too long a marinade will start to chemically cook the meat and decompose its outer fibre. If acid is used, the marination time should be shorter.

Yogurt, also an acid but with a higher pH (about 4 compared to 2 for lemon juice), has a different effect. It adds moisture during marination, and it protects the meat, fish or vegetable from the intense heat of a tandoor or a barbecue.

Enzymes like papaya, pineapple or ginger will also break the proteins at the surface of the meat and help tenderize it.

### Frying (tareko)

Deep-frying is submerging food into hot oil to quickly create a crust on the outside and seal the moisture inside. You can either use an electric deep-fat fryer or a sturdy deep pot and a kitchen thermometer, as I do.

There are simple rules to successful deep-frying:

- The raw ingredients need to be at room temperature.
- Use cold-pressed, unrefined oil. The best oils for frying are rapeseed (canola), rice bran, peanut, mustard and coconut which all have a high smoke point.
- The oil needs to be hot. The ideal deep-frying temperature is between 170°C (158°F) and 190°C (374°F). I have given temperatures in my recipes.
- Plunging your ingredients into the hot oil will cause a temperature drop. It is therefore best to deep fry in small batches and let the temperature come back up after each batch. Turn up the heat if the temperature drops too much, or, add a bit more oil if it is too high, keeping an eye on the thermometer reading.
- Turn your ingredients often to make sure they get an even crispiness, using either tongs or a slotted spoon.
- Listen to the sound of the frying. It starts with an intense bubbling, which is the water from the food turning into steam. It is that steam effect that will slowly penetrate the food and cook it. When the food is cooked, the steam disappears and the amount of bubbles reduces.

- Clean your oil between batches by straining out any crumbs or they will end up burning and transferring that burnt taste to the oil and successive batches of food.

## Wood fire cooking
## (kathko aago ma poleko)

In rural Nepal, meals are cooked over a wood fire. It usually consists of three large stones placed in a circle, with a cooking pot set in the centre over a roaring fire. Long logs of wood are placed between the stones and pushed into the fire as they get consumed to regulate the heat.

The rice is boiled first then covered and set aside to keep warm. The rest of the meal is quickly cooked in woks over the hot fire. The cooler embers on the sides are used to slow-roast tomatoes or chillies, which then get crushed on a flat stone to make chutneys.

With intense heat, ingredients cook fast and acquire a delicious smoky flavour. The food is constantly stirred, making sure nothing burns and the heat gets evenly distributed. Wood fires are also used to dry and preserve meat (see Wood smoking, page 23).

## Balancing (matra malunu)

You will notice that the word "balancing" often appears in my recipes. So does the expression "adjust the seasoning".

Nepali cuisine is an intricate balance of aromas and flavours. My work as a chef is to juggle with four tastes: sweet, salty, bitter and sour.

Sourness is one of the most important tastes as it directly interacts with other flavours. It helps lower the intensity of sweet or bitter, or raise saltiness without adding salt. Using lapsi paste, tamarind or citrus juice as the last flavour in a dish brings it to life and completes it.

# PRESERVATION TECHNIQUES

## Fermentation (amilopan iyaune tarika)

Fermentation is a natural process that is used everywhere in the world. In Nepal, the Newari women are said to have started fermentation to resist the massive destruction of crops ordered by king Prithvi Narayan Shah during his conquests in the mid-18th century.

Fermentation makes food more digestible but also more delicious. The process was further developed and became an important part of Nepali cooking.

Between the cold winter of the high plateaus and the unpredictable length and intensity of the monsoon, we rely on the nutrition and availability of these dried and preserved vegetables.

Another advantage of fermentation is that it improves the nutrition of a plant. For example, bamboo shoots develop healthy probiotics when fermented (see Tama, page 15).

Gundruk and biriya are dried fermented green leaves made with two different techniques. Gundruk is compacted in jars, and fermented in its own lactic acid. For biriya the wilted leaves are coated with urad dal (black lentil) paste and left to dry in the sun (see Sun drying, page 23). The paste accelerates the fermentation process and gives the leaves a tangy taste. It also provides a source of protein. They can be fried in mustard oil with onion, chillies, turmeric and potatoes. Once fermented, both preparations are dried.

You can easily make gundruk using the low setting of your oven, or a dehydrator. 2kg (4¼lb) of leaves (mustard, radish, cauliflower or cabbage) will make about 150–200g (5½–7oz) of dried gundruk. Crush the leaves and stems. Spread them out on trays and leave in the sun or in a dehydrator for 6–8 hours to soften. Roll the leaves tightly and place in a glass jar. Push down on the leaves to make sure there are no air pockets. Cover with filtered water (the chemicals in tap water will weaken the fermentation). Make sure the top is

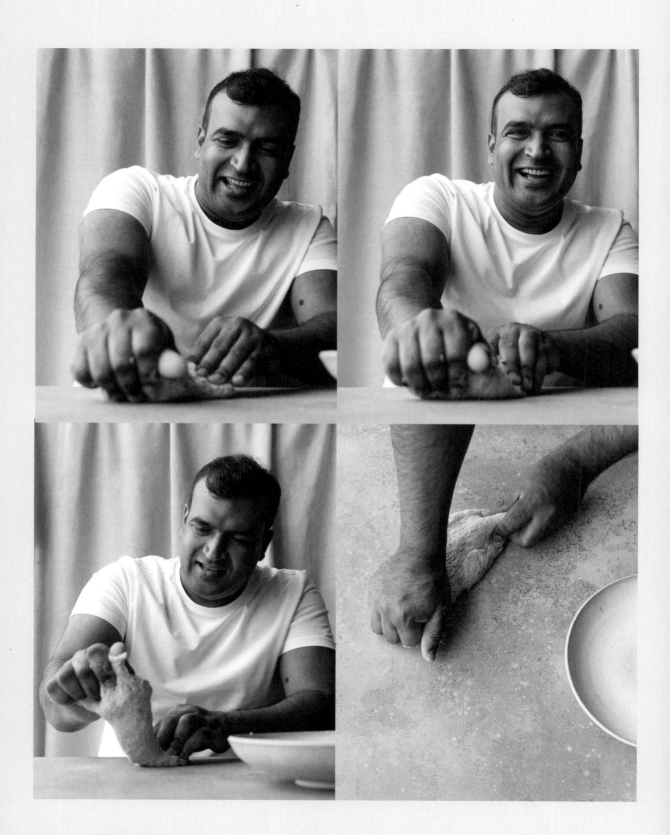

submerged and leave in the sun for 7–8 days, or up to 2 weeks in cold temperatures. Remove the leaves from the jar, dry well and spread on trays. Leave in the sun, in a low oven or in a dehydrator until fully dry. The dried leaves will keep in an airtight container for 6–12 months.

Dahi (yogurt) is another product of fermentation inseparable from Nepali cooking. Thanks to fermentation, milk becomes more digestible and certain vitamins and minerals increase in the process. Dahi accompanies a meal, has its role in soups, curry sauces and bread preparations, is drunk as a refreshing drink and is used in desserts. Yogurt is also a symbol of purity and offered at weddings and during religious ceremonies. In Ayurvedic medicine it is a remedy for gastrointestinal, liver and skin conditions.

Dahi is made by boiling milk and mixing it with curd from a previous batch. The flavour, consistency and fermentation time is different according to where it is prepared. In the hills, they use a wooden pot (theki) and a longer fermentation time, sometimes up to two days. In the Terai, we use clay pots (tankari) and the dahi sets overnight in the heat. The regular production of dahi ensures that the right bacteria are contained in the pots to help turn the milk into a delicious yogurt. If spoilage occurs, the pots are washed with hot water and citron leaves, then re-used for the next batch of dahi.

The Kathmandu valley has an ancient tradition of making sweetened curd which dates back to the Malla period (13th–18th century) called Juju Dhau (king curd). It is prepared by reducing creamy buffalo milk mixed with dark sugar and spices. The reduced milk is poured into an individual clay bowl (kataaro) placed over a bed of rice husks and covered with a blanket to maintain the perfect temperature. After an overnight fermentation, the result is a rich sweet yogurt with a baked custard consistency fit for the kings.

## Sun drying (gham ma sukaune)

This is the oldest form of preservation. It removes moisture and prevents bacteria development and mould growth, while preserving the nutritional value of food.

Traditionally, vegetables are thinly sliced and spread on woven bamboo trays (nanglo) which allow air circulation. Fruits are turned into purée, often flavoured with chillies and spices, and spread on the nanglos to dry into thin leathery sheets that are eaten as candies or rehydrated into purées.

Sun drying is done in the winter when the weather is colder and dryer with still a good number of sunny days. These ideal weather conditions are unpredictable, and farmers often lose part of their produce to rain or insects. Recent agricultural research has seen the development of solar dryers made of drying racks, solar tents and air vents for more efficient drying.

## Wood smoking (kathko dhunwa)

Fish and meat, which take more time to dry than vegetables, are dried over heat to accelerate the process. They are often marinated, the spices having a natural antibacterial effect.

The first drying stage is done over low embers. Some of the chemicals released in the smoke also act as anti-bacterial agents, while the heat will eliminate microorganisms.

Whole, small freshwater fish are threaded on bamboo sticks then placed over embers until the skin is dried. They are moved away from the heat then air-dried in a second stage.

The same double-stage technique applies for meat. Goat, or buffalo, meat is cut into long strips and placed over bamboo sticks to hang high over a low fire, then moved and air-dried until completely dehydrated. We then simply rehydrate it before cooking (see Dry Festive Goat Meat, page 134).

# Snacks & Street Food

**Snacks are a way of life in Nepal and are one of the things I miss the most from home. Nepali people tend to eat two main meals a day and snack in between – this is because, traditionally, the fire was only lit in the morning and at night.**

Snacks, often meant to be eaten cold, are taken out to work to keep you sustained in between the two main meals. Sukuti (Dried Goat Meat Salad, see page 44), is usually served with puffed rice and is a typical example of a Nepali snack. It is rich in protein, can be prepared in advance and is easily transported.

Although snacking began as a necessity and became a habit, snack foods are a most wonderful form of hospitality in Nepal. Guests are treated like family and are always fed well. A cup of Masala Chiya (Masala Tea, see page 209) and a sweet or savoury snack is what would usually be offered. Similarly, we have a tradition of feeding family and friends who visit during festivals. You will find on pages 120–139 that I have included a chapter dedicated to festival food. I have kept it separate because many of these snacks have a symbolic meaning that I wanted to explain, but a lot of the dishes served during festivals and our street foods are connected. Our tradition of snacking, combined with the food served during festivals, gave birth to the culture of street food that is booming today throughout the Kathmandu valley.

Since the 1950s opening of Nepal to the world, and the increased interest in mountaineering, tourism in the country has developed greatly and with it the need for restaurants and street stalls. The curiosity of tourists has also changed over the years, and they are more attuned to authenticity and taste than just nourishment. Online videos and television programmes dedicated to Nepali street food have also contributed to a greater knowledge and increased curiosity in visitors to Nepal.

> **"Snack foods are a most wonderful form of hospitality in Nepal. Guests are treated like family and are always fed well."**

We all know that the best way to experience a country's cuisine is by sampling its street food. Momos are our signature dumplings. In Nepal, we love legends, and the origin of momos is one of them. They were either brought by Newari traders from Tibet, or imported to Tibet through the union of a Newari princess to a Tibetan king. Whatever the history, momos are now Nepali. They are steamed, fried, served in soups or with a chutney. I enjoy them filled with chicken, a hint of lemongrass, ginger and chilli, steamed and served over a tomato and sesame chutney (Kukhura Ko Momo, see page 43).

If momos are connected to Tibet, we have inherited Aloo Chop Sag Wala (Spiced Spinach & Fig Potato Croquettes, see page 30) and Chana Chatpate (Crispy Potato & Puffed Rice Salad, see page 34) from our Indian neighbours, and they have become the most popular potato snacks in the Terai. Chana Chatpate is a totally addictive crispy, crunchy, spicy, sour, salad of puffed rice, potato and fried chana dal. I like it Kathmandu-style, served wrapped up in paper cones and eaten with little squares of cardboard as a spoon.

We have our own Newari version of pizza, called Chatamari (Nepali Rice-cake Pizza, see page 34), a rice and black lentil pancake, topped with spiced minced (ground) meat, egg or cheese. The base is crispy and the topping moist and gooey.

Kathmandu is a colourful maze of bustling streets offering snacks and sweets at every corner and hidden cafés in secret courtyards. Walking down the street, you will not be able to resist the aromas of chargrilled Sekuwa (Grilled Marinated Kebabs, see page 41), freshly cooked Pyaj Ke Kachari (Crispy Onion Beignets, see page 39), or piping hot Masala Chiya (Masala Tea, see page 209). If you ask anyone what Nepali street food is, the answer will most likely be "momos". As much as I love momos, I hope this chapter will help widen your knowledge of our street food. I also hope you will discover how delicious and addictive our snacks can be, enjoyed at any time of the day.

*Following pages:* Huge pans of curries and dals are freshly cooked, and then kept hot, over burners.

*Left:* A Nepali street food vendor cooking at his stall, with piles of freshly fried puri and sweet treats, ready to sell to passing customers.

*Below left:* A coconut seller on the streets of Kathmandu.

*Below right:* Sacred offerings are carefully prepared at Pashupatinath, the oldest Hindu temple in Kathmandu.

# Aloo chop sag wala

*Spiced spinach & fig potato croquettes*

Aloo chop is a popular street food in Nepal – you would go to the market to buy vegetables and get some aloo chop to bring home. I like to give this humble dish a fine-dining twist by serving it with *Karela Ko Chutney* (Bitter Gourd Chutney, see page 174) and introducing a crunchy texture with pomegranate seeds or crushed sweet potato crisps. This recipe is a traditional 'aloo chop' from my birthplace, the Terai region of southern Nepal. The Terai region extends into northern India through West Bengal and Bangladesh, where this dish first originated. We eat them with bhuja (puffed rice, see page 14), fried chillies and chutney.

~

**For the potato cakes**

600g (21oz) boiled potatoes, peeled and grated

4 teaspoons finely chopped fresh ginger

3 green bird's eye chillies, deseeded and finely chopped

1 teaspoon roasted cumin seeds

1 teaspoon salt

30g (¼ cup) cornflour (cornstarch)

⅛ teaspoon ground turmeric

**For the filling**

100g (3½oz) fresh spinach leaves

25g (1½ tablespoons) ghee (clarified butter), or oil

½ teaspoon cumin seeds

1 small red or white onion, finely chopped

2 garlic cloves, finely chopped

4 teaspoons finely chopped fresh ginger

1 fresh green bird's eye chilli, chopped

5 dried figs, finely diced

1 tablespoon chopped coriander (cilantro)

Salt, to taste

Ghee (clarified butter), or oil, for shallow frying

**For the batter**

150g (1½ cups) gram flour

½ teaspoon Kashmiri chilli powder, or medium hot chilli powder

½ teaspoon jwanu (carom seeds)

¼ teaspoon salt

**To serve**

2 handfuls of store-bought puffed rice

6 fresh green bird's eye chilli

Karela Ko Chutney (Bitter Gourd Chutney, see page 147)

~

In a large bowl, add and mix all the ingredients for the potato cakes until well combined. Divide into 12 equal-sized balls. Cover and set aside.

For the filling, blanch the spinach in boiling water, then drain and cool in an iced water bath. Remove from the iced water bath and squeeze dry between your hands. Finely chop the spinach.

Heat the ghee, or oil, in a large, non-stick frying pan over medium heat and add the cumin seeds. When they begin to crackle, add the onion and garlic. Sauté for 5–10 minutes, until the onion is translucent and starts to caramelize. Add the ginger and chilli and continue to cook for 5–10 minutes, until the chilli is soft. Add the chopped spinach, figs and coriander. Cook for 1 minute, tossing all the ingredients together to blend. Season to taste and leave to cool for 10 minutes.

Take a potato ball and make an indentation with your thumb to create a hollow space. Take 1 tablespoon of filling and place into the hollowed potato, bring the sides together, then seal the top to form a ball. Gently flatten the potato ball in your palms to make a patty shape. Repeat the same process to make the other patties, keeping them covered.

Combine all the ingredients for the batter in a bowl. Gradually whisk in 180ml (¾ cup) of water. You want the consistency of double (heavy) cream.

Heat the ghee, or oil, in a large, non-stick frying pan over medium heat. Dip the patties into the gram flour batter and shallow fry them for roughly 5 minutes on each side, until golden.

Serve the patties Terai-style, topped with puffed rice and fried chillies. Offer chutney on the side.

# Chana chatpate

*Crispy potato & puffed rice salad*

You will find many street stalls in Kathmandu and all over the Terai region each selling their version of chatpate. This is a real childhood memory for me. We had five different chatpate stalls around our school. During school break, we would rush to the stalls to get our paper cone of crispy crunchy spicy goodness. Here is my version.

40g (⅓ cup) chiura (beaten rice)

60g (3 cups) store-bought puffed rice

45g (¼ cup) store-bought roasted chickpea snack

150g (5½oz) potatoes, peeled, boiled and diced

2 fresh green chillies, chopped

½ red onion, finely chopped

1 tomato, deseeded and chopped

40g (¼ cup) mouli radish, finely chopped

A handful of fresh coriander (cilantro) leaves, chopped

2 teaspoons Chatpate Masala (Chatpate Spice Mix, see page 189)

Juice of ½ a lemon

1 teaspoon mustard oil

1 teaspoon salt

2 tablespoons crushed instant noodles (optional)

¼ teaspoon Timmur Ko Chhop (Timmur Spice Mix, see page 189)

1 large pinch of store-bought chat masala spice mix, or bire noon (Himalayan black salt), (optional)

Heat a non-stick frying pan. Dry fry the chiura for 4–5 minutes, stirring all the time, until golden in colour. Add the puffed rice and continue to cook for 2–3 minutes, until golden. Transfer to a baking sheet or a large platter, spread them well and leave to cool completely. Once cooled, the rice flakes and puffed rice should be crunchy and crispy.

In a large mixing bowl, combine all the remaining ingredients, fresh followed by dry and then the seasonings and mix well. Just before serving, add the cooled puffed rice and flakes and toss. Adjust the seasoning, adding more lemon, chatpate masala or salt as needed and serve immediately while the mixture is still crunchy.

# Chatamari

*Nepali rice-cake pizza*

Chatamari is a slightly fermented rice and lentil pancake covered with well-seasoned mince (ground meat), egg or cheese. We call it Nepali pizza. You will see chatamari stalls everywhere in the Kathmandu valley. They are cooked on large flat pans, each pancake nested under a conical earthenware lid. The base is crispy and the top moist, hot and fresh.

Chatamari are also a favourite during our festivals (see pages 122–125). Any kind of mince (ground meat) can be used, or even replaced with a vegetarian substitute. Chatamari are always best when freshly cooked. Cook them individually and share while you prepare the next one.

You will need to plan the soaking time for this recipe. Two to three days before cooking, cover the black lentils with water and leave to soak. Then one day before cooking, cover the rice with water and leave to soak.

75g (⅓ cup) black lentils (urad dal)

250g (1¼ cups) basmati rice

½ teaspoon baking powder

1½ teaspoons salt

## For the topping

150g (1 cup) minced (ground) buffalo meat, or any other type of mince

1 garlic clove, finely chopped

4 teaspoons finely chopped fresh ginger

3 tablespoons finely chopped red onion

1 fresh green chilli, chopped

¼ teaspoon Kashmiri chilli powder, or medium hot chilli powder

1 tomato, deseeded and diced

1 tablespoon chopped fresh coriander (cilantro), plus extra to garnish

2 tablespoons frozen peas, defrosted and chopped

1 teaspoon salt

## To finish

2 tablespoons vegetable oil

8 tablespoons grated firm mozzarella cheese

Rub the soaked lentils between your hands to detach the skins. Let the skins rise to the surface and skim them out. Rinse both the lentils and rice then place in a blender with the baking powder, salt and about 100ml (⅓ cup plus 1 tablespoon) of water. Process until you get a thick batter. Leave the batter to rest for 1 hour.

When you are ready to cook the chatamari, combine all the ingredients for the topping in a large bowl, mix well and set aside.

Check the consistency of the rice and lentil batter. It should be thick but easily pourable. Add a little water to loosen if needed.

Heat some of the oil in a non-stick frying pan. Using a ladle, pour about 150ml (½ cup) of batter into the pan and spread it into a 15-cm (6-in) round with the back of the ladle. Using your fingers, drop dollops of the topping mixture (about a quarter) to cover the top. Cover with a lid and cook for 3–4 minutes. Sprinkle the cheese over the meat, when the cheese starts to melt, flip the pizza and continue to cook, covered, for 1 minute, or until the cheese is golden.

When the meat and cheese are cooked, flip the chatamari (cheese-side up) and transfer to a warm plate, garnish with coriander, slice and serve hot. Repeat to prepare and cook the remaining chatamari.

# Kukhura chhoyela

*Spiced chicken salad*

This ancient Newari salad will hit your taste buds with piquant flavours. It is important to make it with grilled chicken as the smoky flavour balances the intensity of the mustard oil tempering. You could also try it with beef, lamb, buffalo or venison instead of chicken, if you like.

700g (24oz) free-range chicken breasts and thighs, bone-in, about 300g (10½oz) cooked chicken

1 tablespoon chopped fresh ginger

4 tablespoons chopped red onion

2 tablespoons chopped spring onions (scallions)

2 tablespoons chopped jimbu (Himalayan leaf garlic) (optional)

1 tablespoon chopped fresh coriander (cilantro)

1 teaspoon ground cumin

1 teaspoon Kashmiri chilli powder, or medium hot chilli powder

¼ teaspoon Timmur Ko Chhop (Timmur Spice Mix, see page 189)

1 tablespoon lemon juice

1 teaspoon salt

1 tablespoon mustard oil

**For the tempering**

1 tablespoon mustard oil

1 teaspoon fenugreek seeds

1 tablespoon chopped garlic

2 dried red chillies, roughly crushed

½ teaspoon ground turmeric

**To serve (optional)**

Chiura (beaten rice, see page 15)

Store-bought puffed rice

Cook the chicken pieces on a barbecue (outdoor grill) at medium heat or on a griddle (grill pan) over direct heat for about 20–25 minutes, turning the pieces often and making sure that the chicken is cooked through. Alternatively, you can also bake the chicken in a preheated oven at 190°C (170°C fan/375°F/Gas 5) for about 30 minutes, or until cooked through. Cover the chicken and leave to cool, then take off the bone and dice into 2-cm (¾-in) pieces. Set aside.

Place the rest of the ingredients apart from the lemon juice, salt, mustard oil and the tempering into a bowl. Add the cooked diced chicken and mix well using two spoons.

For the tempering, heat the mustard oil in a non-stick frying pan. Add the fenugreek seeds and let them get dark brown in colour. Add the garlic and cook for 1 minute. Add the crushed dried red chillies and cook for a few seconds. Then add the turmeric and immediately pour the mixture over the chicken mixture. Mix well, making sure all the chicken pieces are coated with spices and the tempering. Season with the lemon juice, salt and mustard oil.

Serve cold, alone as a salad or with chiura (beaten rice) or puffed rice for a more substantial dish.

# Pyaj ke kachari

*Crispy onion beignets*

When I was a kid, every time we went to the weekly farmers' market, my mother would get me Pyaj Ke Kachari and puffed rice. I still remember slightly burning my lips because I could not wait for them to cool before sinking my teeth in! To ensure they are delightfully crispy all the way through, make sure the oil is at the right temperature before you start frying (I always use a kitchen thermometer). If it is too hot, the beignet will burn on the outside while remaining raw inside; not hot enough, they will not crisp up. You can use cabbage, gourd, or any hard textured vegetable in place of the onion.

These are traditionally served floated in a bowl of Kadi (Sour Yogurt Soup, see page 117), but are also good served with a little Badam Ko Chutney (Coriander & Peanut Chutney, see page 149) on the side.

1 litre (4 cups) vegetable oil, for deep frying

### For the beignets

2 small white or red onions, cut into thin wedges

1 teaspoon garlic paste

1 teaspoon ginger paste

2 fresh green chillies, finely chopped

3 tablespoons fresh coriander (cilantro), chopped

½ teaspoon jwanu (carom seeds)

About 4 heaped tablespoons gram flour

### To serve (optional)

Badam Ko Chutney (Coriander & Peanut Chutney, see page 149)

*A kitchen thermometer*

Heat the oil in a sauté pan until it reaches 160°C (325°F).

Place all the ingredients for the beignet mix, except the gram flour, in a mixing bowl. Start mixing with your hand, then add the 4 tablespoons of gram flour, and continue mixing until the onions release moisture and a soft dough forms. It should be soft but firm enough to hold its shape. Use a bit more gram flour if needed.

Divide the mixture into 12 equal-sized balls. Using slightly wet hands, roll and flatten each ball into a disc.

Deep fry in batches for 8–9 minutes, flipping them halfway through. Drain on kitchen paper (paper towels) and serve warm with chutney, or in a bowl of kadi, as preferred.

# Sekuwa

*Grilled marinated kebabs*

Basantapur is the historic heart of Kathmandu and a hot spot for street food. Just follow your nose and you will find the best Sekuwa kebabs (kabobs). The marinade should be hot, spiked with mustard oil (see page 13) and timmur (Nepali Sichuan peppercorn, see page 17).

To grill the kebabs to perfection, keep them close to the charcoal, turning every 5–10 seconds. You want them to be crispy, juicy and bursting with spicy heat.

1kg (35oz) lamb, buffalo, beef, pork or free-range chicken, cut into bite-sized pieces

**For the marinade**

½ red onion, finely chopped

1 tablespoon ginger paste

1 tablespoon garlic paste

25ml (¾fl oz) lemon juice

25g (1oz) fresh coriander (cilantro), chopped

3 tablespoons jhhau (stone moss), optional

2 tablespoons Mangsahaar Masala (Meat Garam Masala, see page 193)

1 tablespoon Kashmiri chilli powder, or medium hot chilli powder

½ tablespoon ground turmeric

½ teaspoon freshly grated nutmeg

⅛ teaspoon timmur peppercorns, or Sichuan peppercorns

1½ teaspoons salt

4 tablespoons mustard oil

½ tablespoon vegetable oil

**To serve (optional)**

Store-bought puffed rice

Badam Ko Chutney (Coriander & Peanut Chutney, see page 149)

*18 metal skewers, about 15cm (6in) long*

Combine all the ingredients for the marinade in a food processor and blend until smooth. Adjust the seasoning, adding more salt, lemon juice or chilli powder if needed.

Place the meat pieces in a mixing bowl. Add the marinade and toss, making sure they are evenly coated. Cover and leave to marinate in the refrigerator overnight. (You can make the marinade in advance. It will keep refrigerated for 3–4 days.)

Preheat a barbecue (outdoor grill) to medium. Thread the meat pieces onto the metal skewers and grill over hot charcoal, regularly turning the skewers, for 6–10 minutes (depending on the meat), until crispy outside but still moist inside. Alternatively cook, on a griddle (grill pan).

Serve hot with puffed rice and chutney.

# Kukhura ko momo

*Steamed chicken momos with ginger & chilli with a tomato sesame chutney*

Originating in Tibet, momos are now Nepal's most popular dish – we have them for breakfast, lunch or dinner. Minced (ground) buffalo meat is often used in the filling, but you can substitute a meat filling with a mixture of finely chopped vegetables, such as cabbage, cauliflower, green beans, carrots, broccoli and asparagus.

They can be served with any chutney but I like to pair them with a Tomato Sesame Chutney. If you prefer, you can skip making the momo wrappers and substitute these with 20 sheets of store-bought round dumpling pastry.

~

### For the wrappers

200g (1 ½ cups) plain (all-purpose) flour, plus extra for dusting

¼ teaspoon baking powder

1 good pinch of salt

3 tablespoons cornflour (cornstarch), to dust

### For the filling

250g (9oz) free-range chicken thighs, skinned, boned and finely chopped

½ red onion, finely chopped

1 garlic clove, finely chopped

2.5-cm (1-in) piece of fresh ginger, peeled and finely chopped

2 fresh green bird's eye chillies, finely chopped

1 spring onion (scallion), finely chopped

1 small lemongrass stick, finely chopped

1 teaspoon black peppercorns, crushed

1 tablespoon fresh coriander (cilantro), chopped

30g (2 tablespoons) unsalted butter, melted

¾ teaspoon salt

Juice of ½ a lemon

### To serve

Til Ko Golbheda Ko Achar (Tomato Sesame Chutney, see page 151)

Finely sliced red onion and chopped coriander (cilantro)

*A large steamer basket*

~

For the wrapper dough (if making), sift the flour and baking powder onto a clean work surface. Make a well in the centre, sprinkle in the salt and 50ml (3 ½ tablespoons) of water. Start working the dough with your hands. Add another 50ml (3 ½ tablespoons) of water and continue to work until the dough is formed. Knead the dough for about 5 minutes, until smooth and elastic. Cover with a dry kitchen towel (dishcloth) and set aside for 30 minutes.

While the dough is resting, make the filling. Place all the ingredients for the filling in a large bowl and mix until well combined. Adjust the seasoning to taste with salt and set aside.

Make the wrappers. Transfer the dough onto a tabletop well dusted with flour. Roll with your hands into a long cylindrical shape about 2.5cm (1in) in diameter. Cut into pieces about 2.5cm

(1in) wide. Dust with flour and flatten each piece into a circular shape.

Roll out each piece with a rolling pin until you have a circle about 8cm (3¼in) in diameter and the thickness of 1–2mm. Dust the pastry with cornflour between each layer and cover the wrappers with a damp kitchen towel (dishcloth) to prevent them from getting dry.

Take a momo wrapper and wet the edge of the pastry with a little water. Place a heaped teaspoonful of the filling mixture in the centre and starting from one point on the outer edge of the wrapper, make a succession of small pleats, in a circular motion, until you come back to the starting point. Now hold all the pleats together and twist them slightly to seal the opening. Repeat the process to make the rest of the momos and keep them covered.

Transfer all the momos into a large steamer basket. Steam over high heat for 10–12 minutes, until the filling is well cooked. To serve, place a dollop of chutney on a serving plate, place 5 momos on top and garnish with sliced red onion and a sprinkle of chopped coriander.

# Sukuti

*Dried goat meat salad*

Sukuti is the name used for dried meat as well as a popular snack made from it. When a buffalo, goat or lamb is killed, several households will get together to prepare and dry the meat. The flesh is cut into thin strips. The strips are hung from roof rafters, on wooden sticks or ropes, to be air-dried or smoked over a low fire. Sukuti is the meat provision for the hard cold winter.

It goes very well with Chana Chatpate (Crispy Potato & Puffed Rice Salad, see page 34), or serve with puffed rice.

100g (3½oz) dried buffalo, goat and lamb meat, 125g (4½oz) total weight once soaked

2 tablespoons vegetable oil

¼ teaspoon fenugreek seeds

1 dried red chilli

½ red onion, halved and cut into thin wedges

¼ teaspoon ground turmeric

½ tablespoon chopped fresh ginger

½ tablespoon chopped garlic

½ teaspoon salt

¼ teaspoon ground cumin

¼ teaspoon Mangsahaar Masala (Meat Garam Masala, see page 193)

¼ teaspoon Kashmiri chilli powder, or medium hot chilli powder

¼ teaspoon ground coriander

1 tomato, finely chopped

2 teaspoons thin strips of fresh ginger

1 tablespoon chopped coriander (cilantro)

Timmur Ko Chhop (Timmur Spice Mix, see page 189), to season

Store-bought puffed rice, to serve (optional)

Put the dried meat in a heat-proof bowl, cover with hot water and leave to soak for 15–30 minutes. When the meat has softened, squeeze dry and set aside. Discard the soaking water.

Heat the oil in a non-stick frying pan until hot. Add the fenugreek seeds. When they are dark brown, add the dried chilli, then half of the onion wedges. Cook for 2–3 minutes, until the onion softens. Add the turmeric. Stir-fry for a few seconds. Add the ginger, garlic and salt. Stir-fry for 1 minute, then add the soaked meat and stir-fry for a couple of minutes.

Add the ground spices. Stir-fry for 1 minute, then add the tomato, the rest of the onion wedges, the ginger strips and fresh coriander. Season with salt if needed and add a large pinch of timmur ko chhop.

Serve as a warm or cold salad with puffed rice, if you like.

# Meat & Poultry

The great diversity of Nepal's ethnic communities and beliefs becomes even more obvious when it comes to consuming meat. The rules are usually based on health – pigs and chicken eat everything and are more subject to illness, so are therefore considered impure, while wild and free-range animals are seen to be cleaner and purer as they have a better diet.

The ox and cow are sacred for both Hindus and Buddhists. In 2015, the cow was declared the national animal in the Nepali constitution and its slaughter is legally prohibited. Ox and cows are used for farming, but you will also see them wandering freely in streets and around temples. But Nepal is a tolerant secular country, not strictly bound by religious rules, so tourist hotels and restaurants are allowed to serve beef as long as it has not been slaughtered in Nepal.

Buffalos and yaks, also bovine, are used like cows for their milk, ploughing, transport and manure but are not sacred. It gets even more confusing as some communities consume buffalo and yak meat, but certain groups within these communities do not because they consider them too close to cows. Then again, they may be eaten if they have died of natural causes.

Some groups in Nepal consider pigs as impure and would not touch them, but the rules are beginning to relax and for younger generations eating pork has become somewhat trendy. You can often find pork kebabs (kabobs) in the food stalls of Kathmandu – see my recipe for Sekuwa (Grilled Marinated Kebabs) on page 41, which you can make with pork belly, the perfect cut for grilling. Over the years, pig farming has developed into a steady business. Pigs grow fast, they eat everything from corn, flowers and grass, to grains and seeds and can conveniently recycle kitchen waste. They are also the only animal where male and female are both eaten, unlike female goats and buffalos, which are kept for their milk, and hens for their eggs.

---

## "If a life is taken, it should not be wasted. Offals are a special treat and the highlight of festival food."

---

Nepal has a long tradition of hunting. Wild boar was the meat of choice for banquets during the Rana dynasty (see page 59) and still is considered leaner and tastier than pork. Wild boar has been hunted to the point of endangering the species and since 2003, a hunting permit is required. Controversially in 2017, an act was passed to allow wild animals to be commercially farmed.

Goat is considered the king of meat and is consumed by all communities. It is an expensive meat and for most is reserved for festivals and special occasions. Goat farming is well developed in the Terai and the hills, often in parallel with growing crops. When the crop production is low, goat farming offers an additional stable income. Furthermore, goats are easy to raise in areas of low irrigation and harsh climate, and they sustain households with milk and meat. Some of the breeds from the high plateaus, which grow thicker coats because of the cold, are raised for meat and the quality of their wool.

We cook meat on the bone for more flavour and we eat every single part of an animal: head, brain, feet, tongue, liver, kidney, lungs, intestines and blood. If a life is taken, it should not be wasted. Offals are a special treat and the highlight of our festival food, such as Poleko Pangra (Chargrilled Chicken Gizzard, see page 60), which are marinated and barbecued, and tender inside with a crisp, spicy crust.

Any leftover meat that is not cooked or eaten is dried. Thin slices are coated with spices and left to dry in the sun, or above fire embers for a smokier taste. What started as a necessity – to have an adequate supply of protein throughout the year – has become a delicacy. Sukuti (Dried Goat Meat Salad, see page 44) is one of our most popular snacks.

Chicken has become the meat of choice in Nepal, largely due to its low price. The poultry farms supply the urban demands, but in rural areas, village poultry, raised in household backyards, or on the farm, provide enough eggs and chicken meat to sustain families and to generate extra income. My favourite chicken is the red junglefowl (see recipe on page 64). Quail farming for both meat and eggs has also become popular.

*Right:* A black yak rests in Sagarmatha National Park.

*Following pages:* The mighty Himalayas.

# Ranga masu

*Buffalo curry*

Cows are holy and protected in Nepal, but buffalos are farmed for their meat and milk. There are different breeds of buffalos, each adapted to the different climates and geo-conditions, from the Terai to the northern mountains. Buffalo meat has become increasingly popular and is used for curries, poleko (barbecues) and as a filling for momos – see page 43 for Kukhura Ko Momo (Steamed Chicken Momos).

500g (18oz) buffalo, beef or venison, cut into 2.5-cm (1-in) cubes

3 tablespoons mustard oil

½ teaspoon fenugreek seeds

1 tablespoon Samagrah Masala (Whole Spice Garam Masala, see page 194)

½ teaspoon ground cumin

2 onions, finely chopped

½ tablespoon ginger paste

½ tablespoon garlic paste

3 fresh green chillies, tailed and chopped

100g (1 cup) diced mixed (bell) peppers

1 teaspoon ground turmeric

1 teaspoon Kashmiri chilli powder, or medium hot chilli powder

1 ½ teaspoons Mangsahaar Garam Masala (Meat Garam Masala, see page 193)

3 tomatoes, chopped

1 tablespoon chopped fresh coriander (cilantro)

1 tablespoon melted unsalted butter

**To serve (your choice)**

Bhat (Plain Rice, see page 169)

Store-bought puffed rice

Chiura (beaten rice, see page 15)

Roti bread

Wash the meat cubes in cold water to eliminate any traces of blood. The blood is what makes a curry dark in colour. Dry well on kitchen paper (paper towels).

Heat the mustard oil in a heavy-based sauté pan. Add the fenugreek seeds and let them get dark brown, then add whole garam masala. When the seeds start to crackle, add the onions and cook for 4–5 minutes, until soft and lightly caramelized.

Add the ginger, garlic and chillies, and cook for another minute. Add the meat and cook for 3–4 minutes, until well seared. Add the mixed (bell) peppers and ground spices, cover and cook for 20–25 minutes, stirring occasionally to make sure nothing is sticking to the bottom of the pan.

When the meat is tender, add the tomatoes, coriander and butter, and cook, uncovered, for 8–10 minutes, or until the tomatoes are soft.

Serve hot with rice, puffed rice, chiura or bread.

# Bhuteko khhasi ko masu ra lapsi

*Goat curry with lapsi berries*

In Nepal, nothing is wasted and when we cook goat, we use every part of the animal. Here I use a mixture of leg, shoulder and ribs, on the bone and cut in small pieces. This dry goat curry is one of my favourites. I add the popular Nepali ingredient lapsi, a type of sour plum (see page 13), at the very end to enhance the somewhat gamey flavour of this curry. However, you can use tamarind pulp as a substitute.

900g (2lb) assorted goat meat, bone-in, cut into 4-cm (1½-in) cubes

## For the marinade

2 onions, finely chopped

1½ tablespoons ginger paste

1½ tablespoons garlic paste

2 teaspoons salt

2 teaspoons Kashmiri chilli powder, or medium hot chilli powder

2 teaspoons ground cumin

2 teaspoons ground coriander

½ teaspoon ground turmeric

## For the curry

3 tablespoons ghee (clarified butter)

½ teaspoon cloves

2 green cardamoms, lightly crushed

1 black cardamoms, lightly crushed

½ teaspoon black peppercorns, lightly crushed

2 tejpaat (Nepali bay leaves)

3 fresh green chillies, slit lengthways

2 tomatoes, finely chopped

15g (½oz) fresh ginger, peeled and finely chopped

3 tablespoons lapsi paste, or tamarind pulp, see page 17

2 tablespoons chopped fresh coriander (cilantro)

## To serve

Bhat (Plain Rice, see page 169)

Place all the marinade ingredients in a large bowl. Mix until well blended. Add the meat and, using your hands, rub the spice mix into the meat cubes, until they are well coated. Set aside at room temperature for 45–60 minutes.

Make the curry in a heavy-based pan fitted with a lid, heat the ghee over medium-high heat. Add the whole spices. Let them splutter for a few seconds, then add the marinated meat and stir well. Continue stirring the meat over high heat until the juices evaporate and the meat is well seared.

Add the green chillies and 250ml (1 cup) of water, reduce the heat, cover and simmer for 30–40 minutes, until the meat is almost done.

Add the tomatoes and ginger. Cook, uncovered, over high heat for 8–10 minutes, stirring occasionally, to mash the tomatoes. Add 1 or 2 tablespoons of water if needed, to prevent the sauce from sticking to the bottom of the pan.

When the sauce is well reduced and starts to separate (when the ghee appears on the edges of the pan), mix in the lapsi paste or tamarind pulp. Fold in the chopped coriander, cover, switch off the heat and leave for 5 minutes. This allows the meat to finish cooking in its own heat and the flavours to infuse.

Serve hot with rice.

# Tama ra bungur ko masu

*Pork & bamboo shoot curry*

Bamboo shoots are seasonal and only picked from September to December, which is why we preserve them. For the fermentation, only the young shoots are used, thinly sliced, covered with salted water and left in the sun for a week. You can easily get fermented bamboo shoots in a jar from Nepali food stores. They are called tama (see page 15). Here I make use of them in a curry with pork, and serve it with toasted chiura (beaten rice), for a delicious contrast of textures.

You might also like to try my recipe for Tama Ko Achar (Bamboo Shoot Pickle, see page 152).

3 tablespoons vegetable oil

4 tejpaat (Nepali bay leaves)

1 teaspoon cumin seeds

1 teaspoon black peppercorns, lightly crushed

3 red onions, chopped

½ teaspoon salt

500g (18oz) pork neck fillet, cut into 2.5-cm (1-in) cubes

2 garlic cloves, chopped

20g (¾oz) fresh ginger, peeled and chopped

3 fresh hot green chillies, chopped

½ teaspoon ground turmeric

1 teaspoon ground cumin

1 teaspoon Mangsahaar Masala (Meat Garam Masala, see page 193)

1 teaspoon ground coriander

100g (3½oz) tama (fermented bamboo shoots), drained and rinsed

2 tomatoes, chopped

250ml (1 cup) chicken stock, or water

1 tablespoon chopped fresh coriander (cilantro)

## Toasted chiura

2 tablespoons ghee (clarified butter)

¼ teaspoon turmeric

200g (2 cups) chiura (beaten rice, see page 14)

Salt, to taste

Heat the oil in a non-stick sauté pan until very hot. Add the bay leaves, cumin seeds and peppercorns. Fry for few seconds until they crackle, shaking the pan and making sure nothing burns.

Add the chopped onions and the salt. Stir well and cook over medium heat for 10 minutes until the onions are soft.

Add the diced pork and sauté for 5–7 minutes until well caramelized. Add the garlic, ginger and green chillies. Cook for a couple of minutes until they are soft. Stir in all the ground spices, making sure they are well distributed, then add the bamboo shoots and tomatoes and cook for 7–10 minutes.

Once the tomatoes have softened, add the stock or water, bring to a simmer and cook for 10–15 minutes until the pork is cooked through and the sauce has the consistency of a thick gravy. Adjust the seasoning and stir in the coriander. Turn off the heat, cover and leave to infuse for a minute.

While the curry is simmering, prepare the toasted chiura. Heat the ghee in a large non-stick frying pan. Add the turmeric, immediately followed by the chiura. Stir-fry for 5 minutes, until the rice flakes are toasted and crunchy. Season with salt and serve alongside the hot curry.

# Badel ko masu

*Glazed stir-fried wild boar belly*

The Rana dynasty effectively ruled Nepal for more than 100 years from the mid-19<sup>th</sup> century. In contrast to their luxurious Western-influenced lifestyle, the cuisine during this time remained locally sourced. Wild boar, from the Ranas' love of hunting, was often the meat of choice for special occasions, where the boar heads would be proudly exhibited as centrepieces.

Today, wild boars are still hunted in the Terai forests and along the rivers. The meat is usually simply boiled with spices. To give it an Indo-Chinese twist I cook it in a sweet-and-sour glaze. The sharp sourness comes from a small oval-shaped plum we call lapsi (see page 13). I often use lemon as a substitute for lapsi, but in this dish, I prefer tamarind.

650g (23oz) badel (wild boar) belly, or pork belly, cut into 2.5-cm (1-in) pieces

1 tablespoon ginger paste

1 tablespoon garlic paste

1 teaspoon ground turmeric

1 teaspoon salt

8–10 black peppercorns, lightly crushed

3 tejpaat (Nepali bay leaves)

2 star anise

100g (3½oz) fresh coriander (cilantro) roots, roughly chopped

4 tablespoons honey

3 tablespoons soy sauce

## For the stir-fry

2 tablespoons vegetable oil

4 dried red chillies

50g (2oz) jimbu (Himalayan leaf garlic), or chopped spring onion (scallion) greens

2 fresh green chillies, slit lengthways

4 red onions, cut into 1.5-cm (⅝in) cubes

1 teaspoon lapsi paste, or tamarind pulp (see page 13)

Grated zest of ½ a lime

## To serve

Bhat (Plain Rice, see page 169) or roti bread

Place the wild boar (or pork) belly pieces in a heavy-based pan fitted with a lid and add the ginger, garlic, turmeric, salt, peppercorns, bay leaves, star anise, coriander roots, honey and soy sauce. Add just enough water to cover and bring to the boil. Cover, lower the heat and simmer for 1½ hours or until the meat is very tender. Using a slotted spoon, transfer the meat into a heatproof bowl and cover to keep warm. Reduce the cooking liquid until you get the consistency of a demi-glace. Pass it through a fine sieve (strainer) and set aside.

For the stir-fry, heat the oil in a sauté pan over medium-high heat and add the dried red chillies. Stir for a minute or so. You want the chillies to get dark. Add the garlic leaves or spring onions and fry for 30 seconds or so until they start to crisp up. Add the green chillies and the red onions, and sauté until the onions turn translucent.

Add the wild boar (or pork) belly pieces and stir-fry for 3–4 minutes, stirring constantly, until caramelized. If the meat feels dry, add a few tablespoons of the reserved demi-glace, and cook until it is completely reduced. The meat will acquire a shiny glaze. Add the lapsi paste or tamarind pulp and lime zest. Stir well, then check the seasoning.

Serve hot with rice or bread.

# Poleko pangra

*Chargrilled chicken gizzard*

Offal is a delicacy in Nepal. The gizzard is located along the chicken's digestive tract to help it chew food. Because this muscle is constantly in action, it can be tough. Simmering it prior to marinating helps break down the muscle fibres and will give you tender succulent gizzards.

1 teaspoon ground turmeric

2 teaspoons salt

2 tablespoons Samagrah Masala (Whole Spice Garam Masala, see page 194)

500g (18oz) pangra (free-range chicken gizzards), cut and cleaned (ask your butcher to do this)

2 tablespoons melted salted butter

1 tablespoon chopped fresh coriander (cilantro)

### For the marinade

½ tablespoon ginger paste

½ tablespoon garlic paste

1 tablespoon mustard oil

1 tablespoon vegetable oil

Juice of ½ a lemon

1 teaspoon Kashmiri chilli powder, or medium hot chilli powder

½ teaspoon Mangsahaar Masala (Meat Garam Masala, see page 193)

½ teaspoon ground coriander

½ teaspoon ground cumin

⅛ teaspoon Timmur Ko Chhop (Timmur Spice Mix, see page 189)

½ teaspoon salt

### To serve

Hariyo Tamatar Ko Achar (Green Tomato Chutney, see page 158)

In a medium saucepan, bring 1.5 litres (6 cups) of water to the boil. Add the turmeric, salt and whole garam masala, and simmer for 10 minutes.

Add the chicken gizzards and simmer for 30–40 minutes until tender. Drain the gizzards, leave to cool, then cut into bite-sized pieces.

Place all the ingredients for the marinade in a bowl. Stir until well blended. Add the chicken gizzards and leave to marinate in the refrigerator for 2–3 hours.

Remove the gizzards from the refrigerator at least 1 hour before cooking to bring them back to room temperature. Thread the gizzards onto skewers and grill over a barbecue (outdoor grill) or on a griddle (grill) pan for 10–12 minutes, turning them often. Alternatively, bake in a preheated oven at 180°C (160°C fan/325°F/Gas 3) for 15–18 minutes.

Drizzle with the melted butter, sprinkle with the chopped coriander. Check the seasoning and serve with chutney.

# Batain ko masu

*Quail meat curry*

Himalayan quails are slightly bigger than common quails. These wild birds are easy to catch as they fly low, hopping over short distances. But they are less hunted these days as farming them for their meat as well as their eggs has become popular in Nepal. Quail flesh is tender and healthy, containing very little fat and high amounts of vitamin A, iron and phosphorus.

2 tablespoons vegetable oil

1 tablespoon Samagrah Masala (Whole Spice Garam Masala, see page 194)

2 red onions, chopped

6 quails, singed, gutted and each cut into 4 pieces

1 tablespoon ginger paste

1 tablespoon garlic paste

1 teaspoon chopped fresh green chillies

1 teaspoon Kashmiri chilli powder, or medium hot chilli powder

1 teaspoon ground cumin

1 teaspoon ground coriander

1 teaspoon Mangsahaar Masala (Meat Garam Masala, see page193)

1 teaspoon ground turmeric

2 tomatoes, chopped

1 tablespoon fresh coriander (cilantro), chopped

50g (3½ tablespoons) unsalted butter, at room temperature, diced

1 teaspoon salt

**To serve (your choice)**

Bhat (Plain Rice, see page 169)

Chiura (beaten rice, see page 14)

Heat the oil in a non-stick sauté pan. When the oil is hot and a shimmer appears on the surface, add the whole garam masala. Let it crackle for a few seconds, then add the red onions and cook over medium heat for 10–15 minutes until golden brown.

Add the quail pieces and the ginger and garlic pastes, and cook for 4–5 minutes, stirring often, until they start to colour.

Add the green chillies and all the ground spices. Cook for another minute, stirring all the time, then add the tomatoes and fresh coriander. Cook for a couple of minutes, or until the tomato starts to soften.

Add the butter, 250ml (1 cup) of water and the salt, and simmer for about 15–20 minutes, or until the quail is cooked. The sauce should be thin. If you like a thicker sauce, add only half the water. Adjust the seasoning to taste.

Serve hot with rice or chiura.

# Rato kukhura ko jhhoj wala masu

*Red junglefowl curry*

The red junglefowl is a wild chicken indigenous to Asia. I prefer it to chicken because of its stronger flavour – it is particularly tasty in curries. A good substitute for it in this recipe would be guineafowl.

2 tablespoons vegetable oil

½ teaspoon cumin seeds

2 tejpaat (Nepali bay leaves)

2 green cardamoms, lightly crushed

5 black peppercorns, crushed

2 red onions, finely chopped

1 teaspoon salt

1 whole free-range red chicken (red junglefowl), or guineafowl, extra fat removed and cut into 16 pieces

½ tablespoon ginger paste

½ tablespoon garlic paste

1 teaspoon ground cumin

1 teaspoon ground coriander

1 teaspoon Kashmiri chilli powder, or medium hot chilli powder

½ teaspoon ground turmeric

2 tomatoes, chopped or blended to a purée

200ml (scant 1 cup) chicken stock, or water

1 tablespoon chopped fresh coriander (cilantro)

## For the spice powder

3 green cardamoms

5-cm (2-in) piece of cinnamon stick, broken into shards

## To serve (your choice)

Bhat (Plain Rice, see page 169)

Chiura (beaten rice, see page 14)

Heat the oil in a sauté pan large enough to accommodate all the chicken or guineafowl pieces in one layer. Add the cumin seeds, bay leaves, cardamoms and peppercorns. When they crackle, add the onions and ½ teaspoon of the salt and fry on medium heat for 8–10 minutes until golden brown. The salt will help break down the onions and they will cook faster.

Add the chicken pieces, or guineafowl, and cook for about 5–8 minutes until lightly brown, turning the pieces half-way through.

Add the rest of the salt and stir well. Then add the ginger and garlic pastes, cumin, coriander, chilli powder and turmeric. Cook for another 10 minutes, stirring constantly, until the spices begin to release their flavours.

Add the tomatoes and cook for 5 minutes, then add the stock, or water. Reduce the heat and simmer for 15–20 minutes, until the chicken is cooked through.

While the curry is simmering, dry roast the cardamoms and cinnamon shards without oil for a couple of minutes, until aromatic. Leave to cool. When cold, reduce to a powder in a spice grinder. Set aside.

Adjust the seasoning of the curry to taste, then sprinkle with ½ teaspoon of the roasted cardamom and cinnamon spice powder and garnish with the chopped coriander.

Serve hot with rice or chiura.

# Swadilo piro tareko valeko masu

*Crispy chilli chicken*

One of our most popular street foods in Nepal is a direct influence from our Indo-Chinese borders: crispy chilli chicken. It is found everywhere, usually served with soup and chow mein. The success of this dish is all in the technique. First the chicken cubes are coated and deep-fried until golden and beautifully crispy. Then the sauce, prepared in an extremely hot wok, wraps the crispy chicken in a caramelized, charred, umami seal.

It is traditionally served with Amilo Piro Tato Kukhura Ko Jhol (Hot & Sour Soup, see page 68).

~

**For the chicken**

2 tablespoons cornflour (cornstarch)

2 tablespoons plain (all-purpose) flour

¼ teaspoon Kashmiri chilli powder, or medium hot chilli powder

¼ teaspoon salt

400g (14oz) skinless, free-range chicken breasts, cut into 2.5-cm (1-in) cubes

500ml (2 cups) vegetable oil, for deep-frying

**For the sauce**

3 tablespoons vegetable oil

15g (½oz) fresh ginger, peeled and finely chopped

3 garlic cloves, finely chopped

4 fresh green chillies, finely chopped

100g (1 cup) chopped onion

150g (1⅓ cup) diced mixed (bell) peppers

½ chicken stock cube

1 tablespoon dark soy sauce

1 teaspoon white wine vinegar

2 tablespoons cornflour (cornstarch) mixed with 2 tablespoons water

1 large pinch of timmur peppercorns, or Sichuan peppercorns

¼ teaspoon ground cumin

¼ teaspoon Luiche Masala (Chicken Garam Masala, see page 193)

4 tablespoons finely sliced spring onions (scallions)

2 tablespoons fresh coriander (cilantro), chopped

*A kitchen thermometer*

**To serve (optional)**

Amilo Piro Tato Kukhura Ko Jhol (Hot & Sour Soup, see page 68)

~

First, marinate the chicken. Place the cornflour, plain flour, chilli powder and salt into a mixing bowl. Add 4 tablespoons of water and mix until well blended. Add the chicken cubes and toss until well coated.

Heat the 500ml (2 cups) of oil in a large wok until it reaches 180°C (350°F). Deep-fry the coated chicken cubes, in batches, for approximately 7–8 minutes until golden and crispy. Drain on kitchen paper (paper towels) and set aside. Discard the oil.

To make the sauce, heat the oil in the wok over high heat. Stir-fry the ginger, garlic and chillies for 1 minute, until golden. Add the onion and (bell) peppers and cook over high heat for about 5 minutes until charred, stirring frequently. Add about 200ml (scant 1 cup) water and the ½ chicken stock cube and cook for about 3 minutes, until reduced by three quarters. Add the fried chicken pieces, soy sauce and vinegar, and stir-fry for a few seconds, then add the cornflour mix and cook for 1 minute until the mixture is thick enough to coat the chicken and the mixture is well caramelized. Finish by adding the timmur, cumin and garam masala. Adjust the seasoning and add salt if needed, then add the coriander.

Serve the chicken hot and crispy, topped with the sliced spring onions. Offer a bowl of the hot and sour soup on the side, if you like.

# Amilo piro tato kukhura ko jhol

*Hot & sour soup*

Served with crispy chilli chicken (see page 66) or on its own, this hot and sour soup will bring comfort and warmth. As I mention in the Ingredients Directory, in Nepal we use timmur (Nepali Sichuan peppercorn, see page 17) to fight the common cold. This soup is therefore an excellent remedy for regaining strength after illness.

3 tablespoons vegetable oil

20g (¾oz) fresh ginger, peeled and finely chopped

2 large garlic cloves, finely chopped

2 fresh green chillies, chopped

½ red onion, finely chopped

200g (7oz) skinless, boneless free-range chicken thighs, finely chopped

1 teaspoon dark soy sauce

1 litre (4 cups) chicken stock

1 tablespoon white wine vinegar

2 tablespoons cornflour (cornstarch), mixed with 2 tablespoons cold water

Salt, to taste

1 pinch of crushed timmur peppercorns, or Sichuan peppercorns

2 eggs, beaten

1 tablespoon fresh coriander, chopped

**To serve (optional)**

Swadilo Piro Tareko Valeko Masu (Crispy Chilli Chicken, see page 66)

Heat the oil in a medium saucepan over high heat. Add a few droplets of water; when they sizzle, the oil is ready. Add the ginger and garlic and cook for 1–2 minutes until it turns golden. Add the green chillies and red onion and cook for 5 minutes until soft. Add the chicken thighs and stir-fry for 5 minutes until slightly caramelized. Add the soy sauce and chicken stock. Bring to a simmer and cook for 7–10 minutes until the chicken is cooked. Add the vinegar, then the diluted cornflour. Stir until the soup thickens. Add a pinch of timmur, or Sichuan peppercorns.

While the soup is still hot, start pouring in the beaten eggs slowly while stirring. When the eggs form thin strands, turn off the heat. Adjust the seasoning to taste and add the coriander and spring onions.

Divide the soup between four warmed soup bowls, and with a plate of crispy chilli chicken to accompany, if you like.

*Right:* A statue of meditating Buddha.

# Thukpa

*Sherpa noodle soup*

Thukpa is a soup shared by both Nepali and Tibetan Sherpa communities. To handle the freezing winters in high altitude, their diet is heavily based on carbohydrates. The soup is laced with the uplifting warmth of cumin, turmeric and timmur peppercorns. Some cooks add cornflour (cornstarch) or egg white to thicken the soup, but I prefer a thinner broth with my noodles.

100g (3½oz) soba noodles, or egg noodles

3 tablespoons vegetable oil

½ teaspoon hing (asafoetida)

300g (10½oz) free-range chicken breast, finely chopped

½ teaspoon ground turmeric

50g (scant ½ cup) finely chopped carrots

180g (1⅓ cups) finely chopped mixed (bell) peppers

50g (⅓ cup) thinly sliced green French beans

80g (1⅓ cups) finely shredded white cabbage

1 teaspoon salt

800ml (3⅓ cups) chicken stock

2 tablespoons fresh coriander (cilantro), chopped

1 lemon, quartered, to serve (optional)

**For the spice paste**

1 large garlic clove

4 teaspoons finely chopped fresh ginger

4 fresh green chillies, roughly chopped

½ tablespoon cumin seeds, dry roasted

5 timmur peppercorns, or Sichuan peppercorns (see page 17)

¼ teaspoon black peppercorns

1 tablespoon fresh coriander (cilantro), chopped

1 small tomato, deseeded and chopped

Start by making the spice paste. Place all the ingredients for the spice paste except the tomato in a small food processor or electric spice grinder. Blend until you get a paste. Add the chopped tomato and blend again. You should get a smooth spoonable paste. You can make this paste in advance and keep it in the refrigerator for 2–3 days or in the freezer for 1 month.

Cook the noodles according to the packet instructions and set aside.

Heat the oil in a large saucepan over medium heat. Stir in the hing and cook for a few seconds. Add the chicken and cook for 5 minutes, until slightly golden. Add the turmeric and cook for 1 minute.

Add all the vegetables and stir-fry for a couple of minutes. Stir in the salt and spice paste until all the ingredients are well coated. Cook for a couple of minutes.

Pour in the chicken stock, bring to the boil, reduce the heat and simmer for 5 minutes. Add the noodles and cook for a couple of minutes, just enough to reheat them.

Adjust the seasoning to taste, add the chopped coriander and serve with lemon quarters for squeezing over.

# Fish & Seafood

In Nepal, fish symbolize happiness because they swim freely; they also symbolize fertility and abundance as they reproduce quickly. The most common variety of river fish is the carp. With its elegant shape and moving grace, the carp is often used to represent fish throughout Asia. Two golden carps facing each other is one of the eight symbols associated with Buddhism.

Surprisingly, for such a relatively small, landlocked country, Nepal hosts more than 17 major rivers, 70 lakes and a multitude of streams, reservoirs, ponds, swamps and, of course, paddy fields where our rice is grown. Its wide variety of aquatic ecosystems, from the warm waters of the Terai to the cold waters of the high elevations, have produced an abundance of fish species which are completely indigenous to Nepal.

Because of these unique species, Nepal has become a popular destination for fishing tourism. The Babai river in mid-Western Nepal and Phewa Lake in Pokhara are two of the most prized locations. The Babai river is particularly popular for the golden masheer, a giant carp with golden scales, which can weigh up to 50kg (110lb). But apparently the masheer is a clever fish and is not so easy to catch: when they sense an angler nearby, they stop feeding.

In the cold waters, rich with oxygen, fish grow faster. Their constant movement, in order to fight the strong currents, makes their flesh tighter and firm. This is the reason why I use

monkfish and seabass as a substitute for Rohu, our most famous river fish, as I find their textures to be quite similar.

Our fishing industry is starting to grow, particularly in Eastern Nepal, but still remains underdeveloped and does not match the increasing demand for fish. Nepal therefore still imports a lot of its fish. In rural areas, fish is caught locally using traditional techniques, such as rods and traps, or caught by hands reaching under rocks. A favourite activity for the kids!

"In rural areas, fish is caught locally using traditional techniques, such as rods and traps, or caught by hands reaching under rocks."

During the monsoon when the rivers overflow and the currents are high, a profuse amount of small fish get trapped in the fields, making them easy to catch. The paddy fields, ponds, lakes, streams and rivers are also home for freshwater crabs, snails and mussels, which are often stir-fried with spices.

We eat fish at its freshest, ideally when the fish is just out of the water. Instead of filleting fish, we tend to cut it in to pieces, bone-in, and cook it that way for extra flavour. In my recipes, I use fish fillets and I reserve the bones to make a rich stock. Fish is usually prepared simply, mainly fried and eaten with a chutney, or fried and poached in a

curry sauce like my recipe for Machha Ra Jhol (White Fish in Mustard & Onion Sauce, see page 80).

Fish spoils quickly and different methods of preservation are used. These methods are often indigenous, a knowledge that was passed from one generation to the next. We do not make fish sauce or shrimp paste to flavour our food in Nepal, but we use spices instead. Fish are preserved differently according to their size. They can be gutted and coated with turmeric and salt, then hung high over a fire. Preserved this way, fish will keep for about 6 months and are usually then cooked in a curry. Smaller fish are sun-dried and popular in pickles like the Sidra Ko Chutney (Dried Fish Chutney, see page 85).

Climate change, industrialization and human activities are all affecting the health and future of our rivers – fortunately, a national campaign to clean up the rivers of Nepal is helping to raise awareness of the issue.

*Following pages:* A busy afternoon on the streets of the Thamel tourist district in Kathmandu.

*Left:* Jinghe Macha (Fried Breaded Prawns), just one of the delicious ways sweet river prawns (shrimp) are enjoyed in Nepal. See recipe on page 83.

*Bottom left:* Lumbini, a Buddhist pilgrimage site in the Rupandehi district of Nepal, and the birthplace of Buddha.

*Below:* The clear and cold waters of Gangapurna Lake, with a reflection of the snow-covered peaks of the Annapurna mountain range.

# Poleko machha ra jhol

*Spiced monkfish with sesame & tomato sauce*

West of Kathmandu, on the banks of the Trishuli River is the town of Malekhu. This river is famous for rafting and its wide variety of fish, and Malekhu for its fish specialities. If you travel through the town and walk along the river, you will mainly smell fried fish. This is my interpretation of Malekhu fried fish in curry sauce. I like to bake the marinated fish, but it could also be shallow-fried. Serve with a little garnish of Pyaj Ko Achar (Red Onion & Chilli Salad) on the plate.

~

500g (18oz) boned monkfish fillet, taken from the thick upper cut (or any thick cut of white fish fillet)

125g (1 cup) plain (all-purpose) flour

**For the marinade**

2 tablespoons ginger paste

2 tablespoons garlic paste

1 teaspoon ground cumin

1 tablespoon ground garam masala

50g (2oz) fresh coriander (cilantro), chopped

Juice of ½ a lemon

1 teaspoon Kashmiri chilli powder, or medium hot chilli powder

1 teaspoon ground turmeric

2 tablespoons natural (plain) Greek yogurt

1 tablespoon Kasundi mustard (Bengali Kasundi mustard paste)

Salt, to taste

**For the sauce**

75g (½ cup) sesame seeds

2 tablespoons vegetable oil

½ teaspoon fenugreek seeds

1 teaspoon Samagrah (Whole Spice Garam Masala, see page 194)

1 teaspoon finely chopped fresh ginger

1 garlic clove, finely chopped

2 fresh green chillies, finely chopped

1 teaspoon Kashmiri chilli powder, or medium hot chilli powder

1 teaspoon Nepali Barha Masala (Nepali Garam Masala, see page 190)

1 teaspoon ground turmeric

50g (3½ tablespoons) salted butter

3 tomatoes, diced

Salt, to taste

A handful of fresh coriander (cilantro), chopped

**To serve**

Pyaj Ko Achar (Red Onion & Chilli Salad, see page 159)

~

Cut the monkfish into 4 equal fillets or ask your fishmonger to do this. In a large bowl, combine all the ingredients of the fish marinade and mix well. Add the monkfish fillets and delicately mix them in, making sure they are well coated. Place in the refrigerator for 1–2 hours.

Prepare the sauce. First, dry roast the sesame seeds in a non-stick frying pan, until golden all over. Remove from the pan, set aside and leave to cool. Place in a pestle and mortar and crush to a powder. Alternatively, use a small electric spice grinder.

Heat the oil in the frying pan. Add the fenugreek seeds and whole garam masala, and let them crackle. Add the ginger, garlic and green chillies and cook for a couple of minutes until soft. Add the ground spices and butter and cook for another few minutes. Add the diced tomatoes and salt, and cook until the tomatoes get soft and mushy.

Add the ground sesame seeds to the tomato mixture and immediately remove from the heat. Add the coriander and leave to cool slightly. Pour into a blender or a thermomixer and blend until very smooth. Set aside and keep warm.

Preheat the oven to 190°C (170°C fan /375°F/Gas 5).

Spread the flour on a plate. Remove the monkfish fillets from the marinade. Coat each fillet with flour and place on a baking sheet lined with baking parchment. Bake for 15–20 minutes, until the fish is golden brown and cooked through.

Spoon some of the tomato sauce onto a plate and place a monkfish fillet on top. Add a little of the salad on the side. Repeat for the other plates and serve.

# Machha ko jhol

*White fish in mustard & onion sauce*

Nepal has a culture of outdoor cooking. Even riverbanks are used as kitchens. Dried wood can be gathered to start a fire, and a pestle and mortar made with two rocks. The advantage of cooking near the river is eating fish at its freshest, shortly after it has been caught. The traditional way of cooking fish usually includes a short marinade, a deep-fry, then a final simmering in curry sauce. We use rohu fish for this recipe, a very common type of carp in Nepal. You can sometimes find rohu fish in Asian fish markets. If not, perch, or even seabass, is a good alternative. The pungent mustardy base of this curry sauce really suits the sweet taste of freshwater fish or seabass.

~

600g (21oz) river fish fillet, such as carp or perch (or you can use seabass)

Vegetable oil, for deep-frying

**For the marinade**

2 tablespoons ginger paste

2 tablespoons garlic paste

1 teaspoon ground turmeric

1 teaspoon Kashmiri chilli powder, or medium hot chilli powder

2 tablespoons rice flour

1 teaspoon salt

1 teaspoon lemon juice

½ tablespoon vegetable oil

**For the sauce**

3 tablespoons mustard oil

½ teaspoon black mustard seeds

2 red onions, finely sliced

1 teaspoon Sarso Ledo (Yellow Mustard Paste, see page 197), or wholegrain mustard

1¼ teaspoons ground cumin

1 teaspoon Kashmiri red chilli powder, or medium hot chilli powder

1 teaspoon salt, plus extra to taste

2 tomatoes, cut into quarters and deseeded

250ml (1 cup) fish stock, or water

4 fresh green bird's eye chillies, sliced lengthways

A pinch of sugar (optional)

2 tablespoons fresh coriander (cilantro), finely chopped

**To serve**

Kaguna Ko Pulao (Yellow Millet Pulao, see page 172), or Bhat (Plain Rice, see page 169)

Kurkure Pyaj (Onion Crisps, see page 198) (optional)

~

Clean the fish and dry well using a clean kitchen towel (dishcloth), then cut into 4-cm (1½-in) slices.

Place all the marinade ingredients into a bowl and mix into a paste. Add the fish and mix well, making sure all the fish cubes are coated. Place in the refrigerator for 1–2 hours.

Heat the vegetable oil in a wok over high heat. When the oil starts smoking, fry the fish cubes, in batches, for 3–5 minutes. Remove from the oil and

drain on kitchen paper (paper towels). Set aside. (Alternatively, you could shallow-fry the fish in a large, non-stick frying pan using either mustard oil or vegetable oil. Make sure the bottom of the pan is covered with oil.)

Make the sauce in a deep pan or casserole dish, heat the mustard oil to smoking point and add the dark mustard seeds. When they start to crackle, add the onions and sauté for 5–8 minutes over a medium heat, until they become translucent.

Add the mustard paste or wholegrain mustard and sauté for a further 5 minutes. Stir in the cumin, chilli powder and salt. Add the tomatoes and cook until soft. Add the fish stock, bring to the boil and simmer for 2–3 minutes.

Now add the fried fish and green chillies. Leave to simmer for a further 6–8 minutes. Adjust the seasoning to taste with salt (and sugar) and gently stir in the chopped coriander.

Serve at once with pulao or plain rice, and onion crisps on the side, if you like.

# Jinghe macha

*Fried breaded prawns*

Prawns (shrimp) are abundant in Nepal's rivers. The streams and ponds of the Himalayan hills and in the Terai. River prawns are sweeter than sea prawns and their flesh is firmer, particularly when they must manoeuvre against strong currents. We have different sizes of river prawns. The smaller prawns are pan-fried and the larger ones are deep-fried, as here, and served with a chutney on the side.

350g (¾lb) raw king prawns (jumbo shrimp), tails left on

1litre (4 cups) vegetable oil

**For the marinade**

½ tablespoon ginger paste

½ tablespoon garlic paste

1 teaspoon lemon juice

½ teaspoon Kashmiri chilli powder, or medium hot chilli powder

½ teaspoon salt

**For the batter**

80g (scant 1 cup) gram flour

¼ teaspoon salt

½ teaspoon jwanu (carom seeds)

**For the coating**

60g (1 ½ cups) panko breadcrumbs

¼ teaspoon nigella seeds

**To serve**

Til Ko Golbheda Ko Achar (Tomato Sesame Chutney, page 151)

*A kitchen thermometer*

Mix the marinade ingredients in a large bowl. Add the prawns and toss, making sure all the prawns are well coated. Cover and refrigerate for 2 hours, then 30 minutes before cooking time, take the prawns out of the refrigerator.

Combine all the ingredients for the batter in a separate bowl. Gradually whisk in 80ml (⅓ cup) of water. You want the consistency of single (light) cream.

Mix the panko breadcrumbs and the nigella seeds in a bowl. Heat the oil in a sauté pan over a medium heat. When the temperature reaches 170°C (340°F), dip each prawn into the gram flour batter, then into the panko breadcrumbs, making sure they are evenly coated. Deep fry for about 5 minutes, until golden and crisp. Drain on kitchen paper (paper towels).

Serve the prawns hot with chutney on the side.

SERVES 4

# Sidra ko chutney

*Dried fish chutney*

During the monsoon, the rivers, streams and lakes overflow in the fields. Small fish, similar to sprats, get trapped and are easy to harvest. What is not distributed, sold or eaten is dried.

We have different techniques for preserving fish. Medium-size fish are smoked over a fire then hung indoors and left to dry for three to four months. Sidra, which are tiny fish, are dried in the sun for a week then indoors for a further three months. We eat them throughout the winter, adding them to curries or cooked, as in this recipe, as a savoury accompaniment to rice, roti bread or dal.

Any small dried fish sourced from an Asian food store can be used as a substitute to make the sidra.

1 tablespoon mustard oil

½ teaspoon cumin seeds

4 dried red chillies, crushed

1 garlic clove, finely chopped

2 teaspoons finely chopped fresh ginger

25g (1oz) sidra (dried river sprats), or other small dried fish

½ teaspoon ground turmeric

250g (9oz) tomatoes, chopped

½ teaspoon salt

1 teaspoon lemon juice

**To serve (optional)**

Bhat (Plain Rice, see page 169)

Roti bread

Dal

Heat the mustard oil in a non-stick frying pan until hot. Add the cumin seeds and crushed chillies. Cook until the cumin crackles, then add the garlic and ginger and stir-fry for 2–3 minutes.

Add the dried fish and turmeric. Stir-fry for a minute, making sure you get a nice brown colour on the fish. Add the tomatoes and salt and simmer for 5 minutes, until the tomatoes soften. Leave to cool for 1 minute, then transfer to a large pestle and mortar (or a food processor) and crush (or pulse if using a food processor) to obtain a thick paste. Add the lemon juice, adjust the seasoning to taste, adding more lemon juice or salt if needed.

Serve with rice or bread, or as a condiment with dal.

# Vegetarian Dishes

**Nepal has a long tradition of farming. Almost three-quarters of our population is involved in growing and managing its bio-diversity.**

In the tropical and sub-tropical fertile lands of the Terai, we grow a wide variety of vegetables: okra, pointed gourd, jackfruit, bitter gourd, taro, cabbage, cauliflower, pumpkin, tomato, carrot, radish, (bell) peppers and beans.

As you travel up the hills, the agriculture changes. Rice, wheat, maize and lentils are spread over the lower irrigated hills. Millet, pulses (legumes), barley, potatoes and yam are found on higher elevations. The cold and the altitude result in a slower growth which suits root vegetables. The Himalayan potatoes and yam are amongst the best I have tasted. The hills are also a paradise for foragers. Neguro, (fiddlehead fern, see page 14) and sinsu (nettles, see page 15) grow wild and abundant.

Our deeply rooted vegetarian cuisine comes from the diversity of crops and a deep respect for all living things but is also an economic reality: Nepal is one of the poorest countries in the world, and for many households meat is a luxury reserved for special occasions and festivals.

The Himalayan hills are home to over 100 species of medicinal plants and herbs. They are used fresh or dried in pastes, powders and infusions to cure a wide range of illnesses and conditions. The knowledge of these plants is only passed through oral tradition. Scientists

are now recording and studying these species. On my last trip home, I brought back some yarsagumba, a caterpillar fungus which is harvested above 3000m (9850ft) between May and June, and traded at high prices for its therapeutic benefits. It is a tonic – a stimulant to the liver and kidneys which increases vitality. The trade of yarsagumba represents a second income for many mountain communities but, like collecting Himalayan honey from the hanging hives at vertiginous heights, the job comes with high risks: freezing temperature, avalanches, jagged rocks and low oxygen.

## "Our deeply rooted vegetarian cuisine comes from the diversity of crops and deep respect for all living things."

The Western world has taken a recent interest in the consumption of fermented and dried vegetables, yet we in Nepal have been preserving and drying for centuries. The post-harvest loss has always been a concern for farmers: lack of storage, length of transportation to local markets and climatic conditions like an early, or extended, monsoon. What started as a necessity is now a way of life. Roofs covered with drying fruit and vegetables, large pots of fermenting bamboo shoots (tama, see page 15), radishes or bean sprouts, exposed to

the sun are an integral part of our landscape. Drying is a slow, gentle process that keeps most of the nutritional value of produce and, of course, greatly extends its shelf life.

Nepal's most famous dried preserved vegetable is gundruk (see page 21). Sour and pungent, it is one of the things I miss the most from home and I do not hesitate to bring back an extra suitcase of it, or biriya (see page 21) specially made by my friends. We usually serve gundruk in a delicious invigorating Aloo Ra Gundruk Ko Jhol (Fermented Greens & Potato Soup, see page 115). This is typically a home-cooked meal you will not find in restaurants in Nepal. My favourite way to serve gundruk is as a pickle-like-salad, tossed in a piquant mustard oil, tomato and timmur (Nepali Sichuan peppercorns, see page 17) dressing.

Nepali cuisine is one of the healthiest in Asia because it is based on the complex integration of Ayurvedic medicine. Vegetables, herbs and spices are used according to the season and their benefit to the body. The root of our meals is a balanced combination of vegetables, pulses, grains and seeds. From the complex spice mix of Katahar Poleko (Spiced Chargrilled Jackfruit, see page 107) to the rich, silky Karkalo Ko Pat Ko Tarkari (Colocasia Leaves Curry, see page 96), all these resources make an ideal palette for a very creative and unusual vegetable-based cuisine. By sharing recipes that make use of these ingredients with you, I hope to bring exciting new flavour experiences to vegetarians, and meat-eaters alike.

*Left:* View from Ulleri, Bhuktangle, a foothill stop along the Himalayan path in Nepal.

*Bottom left:* A vegetable seller on the streets of Kathmandu, Nepal.

*Below:* Himalayan yam curry is made from a long and short thin root that grows deep into the ground with only a short vine on the surface. See recipe on page 96.

*Following pages:* Nepali women walk through golden yellow mustard fields, carrying willow baskets of leafy greens they have gathered on their backs.

# Chana ko dal

*Spicy chickpeas*

Dal is our comfort food in Nepal and a cheap source of protein. You will find as many different recipes as there are households. Chana dal are the hulled and split kala chana, a small, dark brown type of chickpeas. To give an interesting texture, I process half of the chana dal into a purée, keeping the rest whole. What gives each dal its personality, aside from the type of lentils used, is the tempering. It is important to cook the onions until well caramelized as this will give the dal an extra layer of flavour.

280g (1 ½ cups) chana dal (split Bengal gram)

½ teaspoon ground turmeric

2–3 whole fresh green chillies, tailed and slit lengthways

3–4 cloves

2.5-cm (1-in) piece of cinnamon stick

2–3 green cardamoms, lightly crushed

2 tejpaat (Nepali bay leaves)

1 teaspoon salt

1 tablespoon fresh coriander (cilantro) leaves, chopped

### For the tempering

2 tablespoons ghee (clarified butter), or vegetable oil

2–3 dried red chillies, depending on size or to taste

1 teaspoon cumin seeds

2 red onions, finely chopped

15g (½oz) fresh ginger, peeled and finely chopped

1 tomato, chopped

1 teaspoon Sakahar Barha Masala (Vegetable Garam Masala, see page 194)

### To serve

Bhat (Plain Rice, see page 169)

Puri (Fried Puffed Bread, see page 177)

Wash the chana dal under running water and soak them for 30–60 minutes in lukewarm water.

In a medium heavy-based saucepan, combine the drained chana dal, turmeric, fresh green chillies, whole spices and salt. Cover with 1.4 litres (6 cups) of water and bring to the boil. Lower the heat and simmer, uncovered, for 45–60 minutes, until the dal is cooked through, and the liquid has reduced. Drain half of the dal and place in a blender with some of the cooking liquid. Process to a purée and pour back into the pan. Stir until well blended. The dal should have the consistency of a thick soup. Keep the dal hot.

Make the tempering. Heat the ghee or oil in a non-stick frying pan, add the dried red chillies and cumin seeds. When the seeds start to crackle, add the onions and cook for 12–15 minutes, stirring occasionally, until caramelized. Stir in the ginger and tomato. Cook for 2 minutes, until the tomato is soft. Add the vegetable garam masala, stir well and leave to simmer for 30 seconds.

Pour the whole tempering mixture into the simmering dal, add the chopped coriander and stir until well mixed. Simmer for 3–4 minutes, to allow the flavours to infuse.

Check and adjust the seasoning to taste, adding more salt if needed, and serve hot with rice and puri.

# Maas ko dal

*Black dal*

Although it varies slightly from region to region, you will find this black dal on all the restaurants menus and as a staple in every household. It can be served with rice and bread or even as a soup. Our Himalayan leaf garlic (jimbu, see page 12) is what gives this dal its distinctive flavour. You can find dried jimbu in Nepali food shops, but as a substitute for fresh, I actually prefer to use spring onion (scallion) greens.

100g (½ cup) whole urad dal, or black lentils

¼ teaspoon ground turmeric

1 teaspoon salt

### For the tempering

1 tablespoon ghee (clarified butter)

½ teaspoon cumin seeds

¼ teaspoon hing (asafoetida)

½ teaspoon jimbu (Himalayan leaf garlic), or chopped spring onion (scallion) greens

½ teaspoon chopped garlic

### To serve

Bhat (Plain Rice, see page 169), or roti bread

Combine the urad dal, turmeric and salt in the base of a pressure cooker and add 800ml (3⅓ cups) of water. Bring to a simmer over direct heat on a hob (stovetop), then lock the lid onto the base and bring the pressure to high. Cook for 15 minutes, then turn off the heat and let the pressure drop naturally.

If you are not using a pressure cooker, combine the urad dal, or black lentils, turmeric, salt and water in a large saucepan and bring to a simmer. Cook for 50–60 minutes, or until the lentils are tender, adding more water if required. Using a ladle or a large spoon, stir the dal while crushing the lentils. You want the dal to be thick but still soupy.

Make the tempering. Heat the ghee in a small non-stick frying pan. Add the cumin seeds. When the seeds start to crackle, stir in the hing, jimbu (or chopped spring onion greens) and garlic. Cook until the garlic turns golden brown, stirring all the time. Pour the tempering into the dal and mix well. Cover and leave to infuse for a few minutes.

Serve hot with rice or bread.

# Karkalo ko pat ko tarkari

*Colocasia leaves curry*

Colocasia leaves are the leaves of the taro root and should only be eaten cooked (see page 12). You can find them in Indian grocery stores, rolled in bundles. In Nepal, they grow wild and we pick the young leaves and shoots for this curry. Larger leaves are equally delicious with a unique nutty flavour.

For this curry, you could use some left-over beans from the Quawati (Sprouted Bean Soup, see page 131), or use cooked canned beans.

15g (½oz) garlic, chopped

15g (½oz) fresh ginger, peeled and finely chopped

2 tablespoons vegetable oil

½ teaspoon Samagrah Masala (Whole Spice Garam Masala, see page 194)

130g (4½oz) potato, peeled and cut into 2.5-cm (1-in) cubes

50g (scant ½ cup) finely chopped red or white onion

¾ teaspoon salt

½ teaspoon ground turmeric

200g (7oz) colocasia leaves, tightly rolled together and thinly sliced

1 tomato, chopped

½ teaspoon ground coriander

½ teaspoon ground cumin

½ teaspoon Sakahar Barha Masala (Vegetable Garam Masala, see page 194)

150g (1 cup) cooked mixed beans, drained and rinsed if canned

**To serve**

Bhat (Plain Rice, see page 169)

Place the garlic and ginger in a pestle and mortar or electric spice grinder and crush into a paste.

Heat the oil in a medium saucepan. Add the whole spices. When they start to crackle, add the potato cubes, onion and salt. Stir-fry for 2–3 minutes, until the potato and onion start to turn slightly golden.

Add the turmeric and stir-fry for 30 seconds. Add the ginger-garlic paste and cook for 1 minute, stirring all the time, making sure nothing sticks to the pan.

Stir in the colocasia leaves, tomato, ground coriander, cumin and vegetable garam masala. Add sufficient cold water to cover and cook for 5 minutes.

Add the mixed beans and continue cooking for 2 minutes, just to warm through.

Serve hot with rice.

# Tarul ko tarkari

*Himalayan yam curry*

Tarul (Himalayan yam) is a long and short thin root that grows deep into the ground with only a short vine on the surface. It is a tradition to find the vine and plant a coloured stick next to it. The yam is ready to dig up when the vine has grown up around the stick. Each digger has his own personalized coloured stick. No one would dare steal a root from another digger.

The flesh of the yam is fibrous and perfect to absorb the flavour of a curry. You can also use purple yam or African yam for this recipe.

500g (18oz) Himalayan, purple or African yam

1 ½ tablespoons vegetable oil

1 ½ teaspoons ginger paste

1 ½ teaspoons garlic paste

⅛ teaspoon hing (asafoetida)

¼ teaspoon ground turmeric

½ teaspoon salt

¼ teaspoon Kashmiri chilli powder, or medium hot chilli powder

¼ teaspoon ground cumin

¼ teaspoon ground coriander

100g (3 ½oz) tomatoes, chopped

1 tablespoon chopped fresh coriander (cilantro)

**To serve**

Bhat (Plain Rice, see page 169)

Natural (plain) Greek yogurt

Tama Ko Achar (Bamboo Shoot Pickle, see page 152)

Hariyo Khursani Ko Achar (Green Chilli Pickle, see page 152)

Peel the yam, cut into 2.5-cm (1-in) chunks. Keep in a bowl, covered with water to avoid discoloration while you prepare the rest of the ingredients. Drain and pat dry before use.

Heat the vegetable oil in a non-stick frying pan with a lid. Add the ginger and garlic pastes and cook for a couple of minutes, until soft. Add the hing and turmeric and immediately after, add the yam and salt and cook for 2–3 minutes, until the yam pieces are slightly golden.

Add the chilli powder, cumin and ground coriander and cook for another 2–3 minutes. Then add the tomatoes, cover and cook for 3–4 minutes. Remove the lid, sprinkle with the fresh coriander, cover, turn off the heat and leave to infuse for 1 minute.

Serve hot with rice, yogurt and pickles.

# Kacho kera ko tarkari

*Plantain curry*

The Tharus are an indigenous group who settled in the forests at the foothills of the Himalayas, making the most of foraging and river fishing. They are known for their earthenware, basket-making and the variety of their cuisine. This plantain curry, part of the Tharu diet, is also from my home town.

2 large green plantains, about 360g (13oz) total weight

3 tablespoons vegetable oil

½ teaspoon cumin seeds

1 teaspoon garlic paste

1 teaspoon ginger paste

¼ teaspoon hing (asafoetida)

½ teaspoon ground cumin

1 fresh green chilli, chopped

150g (5 ½oz) tomato, chopped

¼ teaspoon salt

½ teaspoon Sakahar Barha Masala (Vegetable Garam Masala, see page 194)

1 tablespoon chopped fresh coriander (cilantro)

**To serve**

Roti bread

Peel the plantains and cut into 2-cm (¾-in) slices. Keep in a bowl, covered with water to avoid discoloration while you prepare the rest of the ingredients. Drain and pat dry before use.

Heat the oil in a non-stick lidded frying pan. Add the cumin seeds and garlic and ginger pastes. Stir-fry for a couple of minutes, then add the plantain slices and cook, uncovered, for another 2 minutes, until slightly golden.

Add the hing, cumin and green chilli and stir-fry for 1 minute. Add the tomatoes, salt and 200ml (¾ cup) of water, cover with a lid and continue cooking for about 10 minutes, or until the plantain slices are tender. Stir occasionally to make sure nothing sticks at the bottom of the pan.

Add the vegetable garam masala and chopped coriander and leave to infuse for 1 minute.

Serve hot with roti bread.

# Ghar ko jasto ramtoriya ko tarkari

*Home-style okra masala*

Okras or lady fingers become slimy if you overcook them. The secret is to cut them in small rings and cook them quickly. Here is the way we cook okra in our homes in the Terai.

3 tablespoons vegetable oil

1 teaspoon cumin seeds

1 red onion, chopped

1 tomato, finely chopped

300g (10½oz) fresh okras, washed and cut into small rings

½ teaspoon ground turmeric

½ teaspoon ground cumin

½ teaspoon ground coriander

1 teaspoon Kashmiri chilli powder, or medium hot chilli powder

½ teaspoon Sakahar Barha Masala (Vegetable Garam Masala, see page 194)

½ teaspoon salt

1 tablespoon chopped fresh coriander (cilantro)

1 tablespoon salted butter, melted

**To serve (your choice)**

Bhat (Plain Rice, see page 169)

Chiura (beaten rice, see page 14)

Store-bought puffed rice

Heat the oil in a non-stick frying pan. Add the cumin seeds and cook for a few seconds. Add the onion and cook for 5 minutes, until soft and transparent. Add the tomato and cook until soft.

Add the okra rings and stir-fry for 2–3 minutes over medium-high heat. Stir in the turmeric, ground cumin, ground coriander, chilli powder and vegetable garam masala and salt and cook for about 1 minute. Reduce the heat and cook for 5–7 minutes, until the okra rings are soft.

Finish with chopped coriander and melted butter.

Serve hot with rice, chiura or puffed rice.

# Aloo ra gobi ko tarkari

*Dry spiced cauliflower & potatoes*

This is a basic cauliflower and potato dish served everywhere in Nepal. We often eat it on its own with roti bread and chutney or serve it as a side dish with a curry.

The cauliflower should not be overcooked. Start cooking the potatoes first and when they are slightly tender, add the cauliflower. The strips of ginger thrown in at the end give the dish a fresh and zingy finish.

3 tablespoons vegetable oil

1 teaspoon cumin seeds

2 dried red chillies

½ red or white onion, chopped

1 teaspoon ginger paste

1 teaspoon garlic paste

3 fresh green chillies, sliced into rounds

2 medium potatoes, peeled and cut into 2.5-cm (1-in) dice

1 cauliflower, about 700g (1 ½lb), outer leaves removed and chopped into small florets roughly the same size as the potatoes

½ teaspoon ground turmeric

1 teaspoon salt

2 tomatoes, chopped

½ teaspoon Sakahar Barha Masala (Vegetable Garam Masala, see page 194)

1 teaspoon lemon juice

1 tablespoon fresh coriander (cilantro), chopped

2 tablespoons finely cut strips of peeled fresh ginger

**To serve (optional)**

Roti bread

Any chutney of your choice

Heat the oil in a large, heavy-based sauté pan fitted with a lid. Add the cumin seeds and dried chillies. When the seeds crackle, add the onion and sauté for about 10–12 minutes, until golden in colour. Add the ginger and garlic pastes and fry for a few seconds. Add the sliced green chillies and potatoes. Sauté over medium-high heat for 1–2 minutes, then cover the pan with the lid and cook the potatoes in their own steam for 5 minutes, stirring occasionally.

Add the cauliflower florets, turmeric and salt. Stir until all the vegetables are coated with the turmeric. Reduce the heat to medium, cover and continue cooking the vegetables in their own juices for 5 minutes, stirring occasionally to stop them from sticking.

Add the tomatoes and garam masala, stir, cover with a lid and cook for about 5 minutes, or until the vegetables are tender.

Add the lemon juice and adjust the seasoning to taste. Sprinkle with the chopped coriander and fresh ginger strips.

Serve hot with bread and a chutney, or as a side dish.

# Neguro ko sag

*Fiddlehead fern curry*

Neguro or 'fiddleheads' are the curled-up leaves of edible ferns (see page 14). They grow wild and abundantly near our rivers and in our mountains. We pick the furled fronds as well as the younger, more open shoots. Their flavour is a cross between wild asparagus and okras.

300g (10½oz) neguro (fiddlehead fern)

1 tablespoon mustard oil

1 teaspoon fenugreek seeds

2 dried red chillies

1 garlic clove, chopped

1 red onion, chopped

1 teaspoon salt

½ teaspoon ginger paste

½ teaspoon garlic paste

1 teaspoon ground cumin

1 teaspoon Sakahar Barha Masala (Vegetable Garam Masala, see page 194)

1 teaspoon ground turmeric

2 tomatoes, chopped

½ teaspoon lime juice

1 tablespoon melted salted butter

Wash the neguro well under running water. Keep the heads intact and chop the stems.

Heat the mustard oil in a non-stick frying pan over medium-high heat. When the oil is hot, add the fenugreek seeds. Cook them until they go dark brown, then add the dried chillies. Cook for a few seconds. Add the onion and ½ teaspoon of the salt and cook for 7–8 minutes, or until soft.

Add the neguro and cook for 5–6 minutes, stirring occasionally, making sure nothing sticks to the bottom of the pan.

Add the ginger and garlic pastes and cook for a few seconds. Stir in all the ground spices and cook for 2–3 minutes.

Mix in the tomatoes, lime juice, butter and the rest of the salt. Cook for a final 4–5 minutes.

Serve hot with bread, or as a side dish.

# Katahar poleko

*Spiced chargrilled jackfruit*

Jackfruit are extremely popular in Nepal and are used both as a vegetable and a fruit. Ripe jackfruit has a similar flavour to pineapple or mango, whereas green jackfruit has a plainer taste and is perfect for absorbing the flavour of a curry or, as here, a marinade.

Because of its meaty texture, I like to barbecue jackfruit and serve with chips (fries) and chutney – the perfect vegan equivalent to steak and chips!

2 x 400-g (14-oz) cans of jackfruit in water

**For the marinade**

½ tablespoon ginger paste

½ tablespoon garlic paste

½ teaspoon ground coriander

½ teaspoon ground cumin

½ tablespoon Sakahar Barha Masala, (Vegetable Garam Masala, see page 194)

1 teaspoon Sarso Ledo (Yellow Mustard Paste, see page 178), or English mustard

3 tablespoons chopped fresh coriander (cilantro)

Juice of ½ a lemon

½ teaspoon Kashmiri chilli powder, or medium hot chilli powder

½ teaspoon ground turmeric

½ teaspoon dried fenugreek leaves

1 tablespoon mustard oil or vegetable oil

Salt, to taste

**To serve (your choice)**

Badam Ko Chutney (Coriander & Peanut Chutney, see page 149)

Hariyo Tamatar Ko Achar (Green Tomato Chutney, see page 158)

Potato chips (fries), (optional)

*4–6 wooden skewers, pre-soaked in water (optional)*

Drain the canned jackfruit chunks, rinse well under cold water and pat as dry as possible with a clean kitchen towel (dishcloth).

Mix all the marinade ingredients in a bowl until well combined. Add the jackfruit chunks and toss until well coated. Refrigerate for 1–2 hours.

Thread the marinated jackfruit chunks onto pre-soaked wooden skewers and cook on an open grill or barbecue (outdoor grill) until well charred on all sides.

Alternatively, preheat the oven to 190°C (170°C fan/375°F/Gas 5). Arrange the jackfruit chunks on a baking sheet lined with baking parchment and bake in the preheated oven for about 20 minutes, until crusty and charred.

Serve the chargrilled jackfruit with the chutney of your choice and potato chips, if you like.

Note: If you can find fresh green jackfruit, boil 400g (14oz) of peeled 5-cm (2-in) chunks with 2 teaspoons Samagrah Masala (Whole Spice Garam Masala, see page 194), ½ teaspoon Kashmiri chilli powder or medium hot chilli powder, ½ teaspoon of ground turmeric, 25g (1oz) of chopped fresh coriander root and 2 teaspoons of salt for 10 minutes. Drain, leave to cool and marinate as for canned jackfruit.

# Parwal ko taruwa

*Pointed gourd tempura*

Parwals, also known as pointed gourds (see page 14) are widely available in Nepali and Indian vegetable shops. They are about 10cm (4in) long, green and stripy. They are perfect for dipping in this spicy batter which combines gram and rice flours, our Nepali tempura. Japanese baby aubergines (mini eggplants) halved lengthways, or cauliflower florets can be used as well as parwals. Or, to vary the taste and texture, why not use a mix of all three. The batter recipe makes more than needed but will keep well in the refrigerator for three to four days.

~

500g (18oz) any mix of parwals, baby aubergines (eggplant) and cauliflower florets

**For the spice rub**

¾ teaspoon salt

½ teaspoon Kashmiri chilli powder, or medium hot chilli powder

½ teaspoon ground turmeric

¼ teaspoon jwanu (carom seeds)

15g (½oz) fresh ginger, peeled and finely chopped

**For the batter**

60g (scant ½ cup) gram flour

50g (¼ cup) rice flour

¼ teaspoon Kashmiri chilli powder, or medium hot chilli powder

¼ teaspoon ginger paste

¼ teaspoon garlic paste

1 fresh green chilli, finely chopped

½ teaspoon salt

½ tablespoon chopped coriander (cilantro) leaves

300 ml (1 ¼ cups) mustard oil, or vegetable oil, for frying

**For the raita**

200g (7oz) natural (plain) yogurt

½ teaspoon salt

1 teaspoon caster (superfine) sugar

30g (1oz) red onion, finely chopped

30g (1oz) cucumber, deseeded and finely chopped (unpeeled)

1 tablespoon chopped fresh coriander (cilantro)

40g (1 ½oz) pomegranate seeds

¼ teaspoon toasted cumin seeds

**To finish and serve**

Lemon or lime wedges, for squeezing

A small handful of fresh coriander (cilantro), finely chopped

Any chutney, of your choice

*A kitchen thermometer*

Scrape the skin of the parwals to remove any rugosity (wrinkled skin). Cut the baby aubergines in half lengthways. Place the parwals, baby aubergines and cauliflower florets in a bowl. Add all the ingredients for the spice rub. Toss the vegetables until they are well coated with spices. Set aside for 2–3 minutes for the flavours to infuse.

Place all the ingredients for the raita, except the cumin seeds, in a bowl. Stir gently. Sprinkle with the toasted cumin seeds and set aside.

Mix all the ingredients for the batter in a bowl. Whisk in 150ml (⅔ cup) of water gradually, to obtain a smooth batter, the consistency of double (heavy) cream (you may not need all of it). Set aside for the flavours to infuse while you heat the oil in a sauté pan until it reaches 170°C (340°F).

Dip a third of the vegetables into the batter and fry for about 5–7 minutes, until golden brown and tender. Drain on kitchen paper (paper towels). Repeat for the other batches.

Squeeze some lemon or lime juice over the top of the vegetables and sprinkle with chopped coriander.

Serve hot with the raita and a chutney of your choice on the side.

# Sisnu ra aloo ko tarkari

*Potatoes with nettles & spinach*

Nettles grow wild on the high hills, where other vegetables are sparse. We often add them to soups and they are well known for their medicinal properties, good for colds and coughs, to clear eczema, to help detox the body and facilitate good digestion.

Always handle nettles with tongs to avoid any stings. You can make this recipe using only nettles, but I prefer mixing them with baby spinach leaves.

400g (14oz) baby new potatoes, unpeeled

50g (1¾oz) sisnu (nettle leaves), washed and drained

150g (5½oz) baby spinach leaves, washed and drained

1½ tablespoons ghee (clarified butter)

1 teaspoon cumin seeds

2 dried red chillies

100g (generous 1 cup) finely chopped red onion

2 large garlic cloves, finely chopped

15g (½oz) fresh ginger, peeled and finely chopped

2 teaspoons lemon juice

½ teaspoon salt

A handful of fresh coriander (cilantro), chopped

Boil the baby potatoes in salted water for 20 minutes, or until soft. Drain and leave to cool. When they are cool enough to handle, remove the skin and cut them in half.

Blanch the nettle leaves in hot water for about 5 minutes, then remove them with tongs, placing them directly into an iced water bath. When the leaves have cooled down, remove them from the water into a sieve (strainer). Blanch the spinach for 30 seconds and cool in the same way (you will need to add more ice to your water bath). Transfer the drained nettles and spinach to a blender or a food processor and blend into a smooth slightly liquid purée. Add 3–4 tablespoons of water if needed.

Heat the ghee in a sauté pan over high heat. Add the cumin seeds and the dried red chillies. Cook until they crackle, then add the onions and sauté for 5–6 minutes, until golden brown. Add the garlic and ginger and cook for 2–3 minutes.

Add the nettle and spinach purée and cook for a couple of minutes, stirring all the time. When the mixture is simmering, add the potatoes and cook for another couple of minutes until the potatoes are warm. Season with the lemon juice, add more salt and sprinkle over the chopped coriander. Serve hot.

# Karela bhareko

*Stuffed bitter gourd*

Karela (bitter gourd, see page 13) is a unique vegetable with a thick skin that can vary from knobbly to spiky. The seedy centre is scooped out and discarded and only the skin is cooked. It is often overlooked because of its intense bitterness. This is my favourite way to prepare it, which is one of my mother's best recipes – stuffed and served with a spicy tomato-based curry sauce.

~

1 teaspoon yellow mustard seeds (soaked overnight, see method)

4 karela (bitter gourds)

2 tablespoons vegetable oil

**For the stuffing**

4 teaspoons finely chopped fresh ginger

1 garlic clove, chopped

2 tablespoons chopped fresh mango flesh, or 1 tablespoon amchur (mango powder)

3 tablespoons raisins

2 tablespoons fresh coriander (cilantro), chopped

3 fresh green chillies, chopped

1 teaspoon ground turmeric

1 teaspoon ground cumin

2 tablespoons sesame seeds, toasted

½ teaspoon salt

**For the sauce**

1 tablespoon mustard oil

1 teaspoon cumin seeds

1½ teaspoons finely chopped fresh ginger

1½ teaspoons finely chopped garlic

1 red onion, finely chopped

2 tomatoes, chopped

1 fresh green chilli, tailed and slit opened

1 teaspoon Kashmiri chilli powder, or medium hot chilli powder

1 teaspoon ground cumin

1 teaspoon ground coriander

1 teaspoon Sakahar Barha Masala (Vegetable Garam Masala, see page 194)

½ teaspoon salt

1 tablespoon chopped fresh coriander (cilantro)

**To serve**

Bhat (Plain Rice, see page 169), or roti bread

*Kitchen string (twine)*

~

Put the mustard seeds in a small bowl, cover with 1 tablespoon of water and leave to soak overnight. The next day, the seeds will have absorbed the water. Place them in a pestle and mortar and grind into a paste. Set aside.

Using a sharp knife, make a deep slit lengthways in each bitter gourd. You want to make a pocket and not pierce them all the way through. Using a teaspoon, scoop out and discard the seeds and white flesh. Set aside.

Place all the ingredients for the stuffing in a food processor and pulse a few times. You want the paste to remain chunky and not too fine. Adjust the seasoning to taste. Fill each bitter gourd with some of the stuffing mixture. Tie a couple of lengths of kitchen string around each one to make sure the stuffing does not escape during cooking.

Heat the oil in a non-stick frying pan. Add the stuffed gourds and cook covered, over low heat, for 20 minutes, turning them every 4–5 minutes. Add a little bit of water if needed. Alternatively, brush them lightly with oil and bake at 180°C (160°C fan/ 350°F/Gas 4) for 25 minutes.

While the gourds are cooking, prepare the curry sauce. Heat the oil in a medium, non-stick frying pan. Add the cumin seeds. When they crackle, add the ginger and garlic and cook for 1 minute, until slightly golden. Add the onion and cook for about 7 minutes, until lightly caramelized.

Stir in the tomatoes, green chilli and all the ground spices. Cook for 5–10 minutes, until the tomatoes have completely softened. Add the salt, chopped coriander and mustard seed paste. Cook for a couple of minutes. Using a hand blender or a food processor, blend the sauce until smooth. Adjust the seasoning to taste. Add the gourds to the sauce and cook for another 3–4 minutes.

Serve hot with rice or bread.

# Aloo ra gundruk ko jhol

*Fermented greens & potato soup*

During the cold winter of the high plateaux and the monsoon in the Terai, fresh vegetables are often unavailable for many months. Fermenting and drying leafy greens in the Autumn (Fall) is a way of getting healthy restorative meals during these difficult times. These leaves, called gundruk (see page 12), are often incorporated in soups, such as this one.

50g (2oz) gundruk
  (dried fermented greens)

3 tablespoons vegetable oil,
  or mustard oil

1 red onion, finely chopped

1 large potato, peeled and diced

1 teaspoon ginger paste

1 teaspoon garlic paste

1 teaspoon Kashmiri chilli powder,
  or medium hot chilli powder

1 teaspoon ground cumin

1 teaspoon ground turmeric

2 tomatoes, chopped

¼ teaspoon Timmur Ko Chhop
  (Timmur Spice Mix, see page 189)

600ml (2½ cups) vegetable stock,
  or water

Salt, to taste

**To serve**

Bhat (Plain rice, see page 169),
  or roti bread

Soak the dried gundruk in a bowl of warm water for 30 minutes. Drain and squeeze between your hands to remove any excess water. Chop finely. Heat half of the oil in a non-stick frying pan and sauté the gundruk for 2–3 minutes until fragrant and slightly crispy. Transfer to a heatproof bowl and reserve.

Add the rest of the oil to a large saucepan and cook the onion over medium heat for about 10 minutes until golden. Add the diced potato and cook for 3–4 minutes.

Add the fried gundruk and sauté for 1 minute. Stir in the ginger and garlic pastes and the ground spices and cook for another minute. Add the chopped tomatoes and timmur ko chhop and cook for a few more minutes until the tomatoes soften.

Add the vegetable stock or water, bring to the boil, then lower the heat and simmer, uncovered, for 10–15 minutes, or until the potatoes are cooked. Adjust the seasoning to taste with salt.

Serve hot with rice or bread.

# Kadi

*Sour yogurt soup*

Making kadi is a clever way to use up left over yogurt that has gone sour. In fact, the yogurt acidity is crucial for the authenticity of the taste. If you are using fresh yogurt, add a squeeze of lemon juice at the end. (See Dahi on page 22 for more about the use of yogurt in Nepali cuisine.)

We often add Pyaj Ke Kachari (Crispy Onion Beignets, see page 39), to this yogurt soup (as pictured here) and serve it with rice or roti bread on the side.

100g (scant ½ cup) natural (plain) yogurt, soured

15g (4 teaspoons) gram flour

¼ teaspoon ground turmeric

1 ½ teaspoons finely chopped fresh ginger

¾ teaspoon salt

### For the tempering

2 tablespoons vegetable oil

½ teaspoon fenugreek seeds

¼ teaspoon cumin seeds

¼ teaspoon mustard seeds

2 dried red chillies, crushed

4 fresh curry leaves

½ teaspoon ground cumin

⅛ teaspoon amchur (mango powder)

⅛ teaspoon hing (asafoetida)

### To serve (your choice)

6 Pyaj Ke Kachari (Crispy Onion Beignets, see page 39)

Bhat (Plain Rice, see page 169)

Roti bread

Lemon wedges, for squeezing (optional)

Combine the yogurt, gram flour, turmeric, ginger and salt in a mixing bowl. Gradually whisk in 350ml (1 ½ cups) of water until everything is well blended and the mixture is smooth.

Pour the yogurt mixture into a saucepan over low heat, and heat, whisking occasionally, until thickened. It should have the consistency of a thick soup.

While the yogurt is cooking, make the tempering. Heat the oil in a small, non-stick frying pan over medium heat. When hot, add the fenugreek seeds and cook until they darken. Add the cumin and mustard seeds and cook until they crackle. Add the dried red chillies and curry leaves and stir-fry for 1 minute. Add the ground cumin, amchur and hing and immediately remove from the heat, making sure they do not burn.

Whisk the tempering into the yogurt soup and adjust the seasoning.

If you are serving this with Pyaj Ke Kachari, fry them at the last minute and add to the warm yogurt soup.

Serve with rice and roti bread and lemon wedges for squeezing, if you like.

# Aloo ko tarkari

*Potato curry*

Aloo Ko Tarkari (potato curry) is so often eaten with puri, that I have combined the two recipes for you here. Puri are also served alongside other dishes, such as Chana Ko Dal (Spicy Chickpeas, page 93). The puri here are vegan, but see page 177 for an alternative recipe, with the option of ghee (clarified butter), and if you want to make them without the potato curry.

~

## For the puri (makes 20)

500g (3¾ cups) plain (all-purpose) flour or roti (chapati) flour, or an equal mixture of both

2 teaspoons salt

1 tablespoon vegetable oil, for working into the dough

1 litre (4 cups) vegetable oil, for deep-frying

2 tablespoons vegetable oil, for rolling

## For the potato curry

2 ½ tablespoons vegetable oil

1 teaspoon fenugreek seeds

½ teaspoon cumin seeds

½ teaspoon nigella seeds

½ teaspoon garlic paste

½ teaspoon ginger paste

500g (18oz) red-skinned waxy potatoes, unpeeled and diced

½ teaspoon salt, or to taste

2 dried hot red chillies, crushed

¼ teaspoon Kashmiri chilli powder, or medium hot chilli powder

½ teaspoon Sakahar Barha Masala (Vegetable Garam Masala, see page 194)

½ teaspoon ground turmeric

500ml (2 cups) vegetable stock, or water

*A kitchen thermometer*

~

First, make the puri dough. Combine the flour and salt into a bowl. Add the 1 tablespoon of oil and, using your fingers, work the oil into the flour until well incorporated. Make a well in the flour and measure out 250ml (1 cup) of water. Add some of the water into the well and start mixing the dough, gradually adding the remaining water, a little at a time, until a firm dough forms. Knead the dough well with your hands for about 10 minutes until soft and elastic.

Cover with a clean damp cloth and set aside for 15 minutes. Divide the dough into 20 pieces and keep them covered.

Make the potato curry. Heat the oil in a medium non-stick frying pan. Add the fenugreek seeds and let them crackle until they turn dark brown.

Add the cumin and nigella seeds. Cook them for a few seconds just until they crackle. Add the garlic and ginger pastes, potato cubes, salt, crushed red chillies and all the ground spices. Sauté for a couple of minutes, until the potatoes are well coated with oil and spices. Add the vegetable stock or water, bring the mixture to the boil, and then turn down the heat to low.

Simmer on low heat for about 30 minutes until most of the liquid has been absorbed and the potatoes are soft. When the potatoes are soft enough, start stirring them while lightly crushing them with a spatula. You want the potatoes to absorb all the liquid and to have some chunkiness and texture. When they are thick and glossy from the juices, they are ready.

While the potatoes are cooking, fry the puri. Heat the oil in a deep sauté pan until it reaches 190°C (375°F). Roll one of the dough pieces in your hand to make a smooth ball. Apply a little oil on the dough ball and roll it out on an oiled surface with a rolling pin to obtain a 10-cm (4-in) disc. Repeat with the other dough balls. Keep the discs covered with a wet cloth.

Place a puri in the hot oil. When it rises to the surface, press it down very gently into the oil with a skimmer. The puri will start puffing up. Flip it over and cook for a few seconds. When the puri are crisp and golden brown – this should take a couple of minutes on each side – remove from the oil and place on kitchen paper (paper towels) to drain.

Serve the potato curry hot with the crisp puri on the side.

# Festival
# Food

In Nepal, we celebrate more than 50 festivals each year across a range of communities and religions. These festivals define our culture and spiritual beliefs, and connect us to the seasons and harvests, to what we eat, and to our family and friends.

Festivals follow the rhythm of the moon and therefore the date when each festival starts is different every year according to the monthly western calendar.

Coming together to share a meal is often a key part of festivities – I have listed here a few of the major festivals we celebrate in Nepal, alongside some of the most popular recipes connected with each of them.

## FEBRUARY – MARCH

**Fagu Purnima** is our festival of spring, colours and love, rebirth after the winter, and, as the legend goes, the victory of Lord Vishnu over the evil king Hiranyakashipu.

Pigments of all colours are thrown in the air and a 10m (32ft) bamboo trunk is erected and set on fire to start the festival.

Fagu Purnima is a festival of joy, music, dancing and sweets! My favourite dish is Malpuwa Ra Rabri (see page 129), an irresistible pancake, partly made with rice flour, drenched in syrup and served with rabri, which is a creamy saffron sauce, obtained by patiently reducing milk to a creamy consistency.

## AUGUST

**Janai Purnima** is a spiritual festival celebrated by people of different cultures, religions and beliefs. Janai means holy thread and Purnima full moon. During Janai Purnima, we pray, visit our temples, Brahmin priests renew their Janai and the shamans gather in their sacred grounds. Janai is a symbol of purity, blessing and protection.

In the Terai, on that same day, we celebrate Raksha Bandhan, exchanging wishes of prosperity and promises of protection within the family. It is a time for family gathering where Quawati (see page 131), a wholesome soup made with nine types of beans, is served to keep the body strong and healthy.

## SEPTEMBER – OCTOBER

**Dashain** is the most important Hindu festival in Nepal: the victory of the goddess Durga over the demon Mahishasura. The fight lasted nine days and Mahishasura was defeated on the tenth. This festival lasts 15 days. The last five days are dedicated to the celebration of Durga's victory.

Because of the long holiday, it is a time for Nepali people scattered around the world to return home and celebrate. It is a joyous moment of gathering

and, of course, good food. Selroti (see page 137) is one of the two traditional recipes prepared during the Dashain festival. It is a ring-shaped, sweet rice bread, expertly deep-fried in a wok of hot oil. Crispy with a soft, doughy centre, this bread is extremely popular and has become an iconic street food.

Dashain is also associated with feasting on meat. The meat of choice is goat, slowly cooked with spices until tender and succulent, so the second recipe we prepare to eat is Pakku (see page 134).

*Opposite page:* People gather at the Nyatapola temple in Bhaktapur to celebrate Maghe Sankranti.

*Below:* Sacred dance being performed in the Chiwong Monastery during Mani Rimdu – a 19-day festival most popular with Sherpa communities to celebrate the founding of Buddhism.

### OCTOBER – NOVEMBER

**Tihar** is a five-day Hindu festival: the festival of lights. Tihar encompasses many celebrations: the celebration of sacred animals like crows, dogs, cows and oxen, the worship of Lakshmi, the goddess of wealth, the celebration of one's own existence, and praying for the success and longevity of siblings. We decorate our homes with oil lamps inside and out, and our courtyards with coloured rice, dry flour, coloured sand or flower petals.

Selroti (see pages 123 and 137) are baked in the morning, a portion reserved for offerings and the rest served later often with Aloo Ko Achar (Potato Pickle, see page 163).

### NOVEMBER

**Chhath Parva**, is celebrated in the Eastern Terai and dedicated to the worship of the Sun God. During Chhath Parva, we gather, take baths in rivers and ponds and pray to the rising and setting sun. It is a collective prayer-seeking for protection and prosperity for everybody.

Two of the traditional dishes for this festival are Sandheko Bhogate and Khajuria. Sandheko Bhogate (see page 132) is a pungent but refreshing pomelo and yogurt salad, laced with spices and mustard oil. Khajuria (see page 215) is a fried cookie, made with ghee, coconut and raisins. It is beautifully crisp, crumbly and buttery.

### DECEMBER

**Yomari Punhi** is the most popular of the Newari festivals and is celebrated during the full moon in December. The festival is dedicated to Annapurna, the goddess of grain. We thank her for the rice harvest. Processions in traditional outfits, singing and dancing are organized by the Newari communities.

Yomari (see page 138) is a steamed rice dumpling with a sweet filling and it is the highlight of the festival. The bread is shaped into a fish or a shrine, or sometimes figurines. Preparing yomari is intricate and usually involves the whole family. Traditionally, it is filled with toffee molasses and sesame seeds to give the body energy and warmth.

## JANUARY

**Maghe Sankranti** happens in the middle of January and corresponds to the winter solstice and the start of longer days. It is our new year celebration with family and friends, full of eating, drinking and joy.

Til Ko Ladoo (see page 127) is the traditional sweet. It is a crispy ball of sesame seeds and jaggery toffee. Eating sesame seeds, ghee, sweet potatoes and yam is believed to keep the body healthy.

*Opposite page:* Temples in Durbar Square in the ancient Newar city Bhaktapur – the so-called City of Festivals.

*Below:* Offerings made to Hindu gods during a traditional Hindu Nepali wedding will include the festival treat Selroti (fried ring bread).

# Til ko ladoo

*Sesame & jaggery balls*

Mid-January, a few weeks after the winter solstice, is the celebration of the Maghe Sankranti festival which coincides with the harvesting of sesame seeds. One of the food preparations for this festival is sesame and gud (jaggery) balls. Sesame seeds are linked to prosperity and longevity, the perfect symbol for a festival which celebrates the end of winter and the start of a new year. They are also packed with good fats and are believed to provide warmth to the body in Ayurvedic medicine.

In the Terai, where I am from, a similar recipe is made with puffed rice, or chiura (beaten rice) and is called Til Ke Lai.

150g (1 generous cup) white sesame seeds

110g (½ cup) gud (jaggery), chopped

2 tablespoons ghee (clarified butter), melted

*A kitchen thermometer*

*A baking sheet, lined with baking parchment*

Heat a non-stick frying pan over medium heat. Toast the sesame seeds for 6–7 minutes, until golden brown. Transfer to a plate and leave to cool.

In the same pan, melt the gud with ½ tablespoon of water and cook over medium heat until it reaches the soft ball stage (114°C/237°F). The gud will have thickened and look like glue. If you drop a bit in cold water and rub it between two fingers, it will be sticky.

Take the pan off the heat, add the sesame seeds and mix quickly before the jaggery caramel sets.

When the mixture is cool enough to handle but while it is still malleable, apply a little melted ghee to your hands and roll 1 tablespoon of the mixture between your palms to form a ball. Set the balls on the prepared baking sheet. Repeat with the rest of the mixture.

Serve at room temperature. They will keep for 1 week in an air-tight container.

# Terai malpuwa ra rabri

*Syrupy pancakes with saffron creamy milk*

Holi is the festival of joy and colours, the celebration of the beginning of spring. We bless each other by throwing bright coloured water and pigments. It is a tradition to serve Malpuwa and Rabri during this festival. These crispy and delicate pancakes, drenched in syrup and topped with creamy saffron milk, are served all year round in the Terai, and particularly in the city of Janakpur.

~

**For the pancake batter**

200g (1 ½ cups) plain (all-purpose) flour

50g (⅓ cup) rice flour

25g (5 tablespoons) milk powder

½ teaspoon baking powder (optional)

½ teaspoon fennel seeds, plus
   1 teaspoon extra for cooking

2¾ tablespoons desiccated (shredded)
   coconut, plus 1 tablespoon extra
   for cooking

250ml (1 cup) whole (full-fat) milk,
   warmed

**For the rabri**

800ml (3⅓ cups) whole (full-fat) milk
⅛ teaspoon saffron threads, diluted in
   1 tablespoon warmed milk

**For the syrup**

250g (1 ¼ cups) caster (superfine) sugar

8–10 saffron threads

**To finish and serve**

6 tablespoons ghee (clarified butter)

2 tablespoons chopped pistachios

2–3 small squares of edible gold
   leaf (optional)

Combine all the ingredients for the pancake batter in a mixing bowl, except the milk. Baking powder will make the pancakes lighter but it is optional. Gradually add the warm milk, whisking constantly until you obtain a smooth batter with the consistency of double (heavy) cream. Set aside for about 1 hour at room temperature while you make the rabri.

Pour the milk for the rabri into a deep, non-stick frying pan. Bring to a simmer and cook for about 1 hour, stirring occasionally to make sure it doesn't catch and burn at the bottom. When a first skin forms on the surface of the milk, carefully drag it with a spatula pushing it up the edges of the frying pan. It will stick to the edges. Repeat every time a skin forms. You want to collect and keep the skins. When the milk has reduced to the consistency of double cream, scrape all the skins back into the pan. They will give the rabri a lumpy texture which is very traditional. Stir in the saffron and keep warm while you prepare the rest of the dessert.

To make the syrup, mix the sugar and 150ml (⅔ cup) of cold water in a heavy-based saucepan. Place over low heat and stir until the sugar is dissolved. Bring to the boil and cook for 3–4 minutes, until the syrup is bubbly and thickened. Remove from the heat, stir in the saffron threads and set aside.

Heat the ghee in a large, non-stick frying pan. Pour a small ladleful of batter, about 50ml (3 ½ tablespoons) into the hot ghee. The batter will naturally spread into an oval shape. Fry 3–4 ladlefuls of batter at a time. Sprinkle a few extra fennel seeds and a little desiccated coconut over the top of each pancake. Cook for a couple of minutes, splashing some of the hot ghee over the tops to cook them. When the pancakes are golden underneath, flip them over and cook until golden. Remove to a plate and keep warm. Repeat until you run out of batter.

Pile up the pancakes on plates (serving 4 per person), drizzle with some syrup and garnish with pistachios and a few flakes of gold leaf, if using. Spoon some rabri on each serving plate, or serve it on the side and let each guest pour some over their own portion.

# Quawati

*Sprouted bean soup*

Janai Purnima, also called the 'thread festival', starts on the first full moon of August. The janai is the thread worn around the wrist of believers and around the chest of Hindu priests, a symbol of purity and blessing from the gods. A new thread is tied every year during this festival.

The Newars of Kathmandu valley call this festival Guhni Punhia. This is a time of gathering for family and friends, celebrated with a hearty soup made with a mixture of seven to nine beans. In Nepal, we always sprout beans, making them more digestible and wholesome. The soup is believed to give the body strength during the monsoon months. In the heat of the summer months, the beans will sprout overnight. In a colder climate, they may need to be soaked for two to three days and kept in a warm place to encourage sprouting.

200g (1¼ cups) mixed dried beans (such as mung beans, black urad, soybean, black-eyed peas, dried peas, haricot beans, fava beans, chickpeas, red kidney beans)

**For the tempering**

2 tablespoons ghee (clarified butter)

1 tablespoon jwanu (carom seeds)

2 tejpaat (Nepali bay leaves)

1 red onion, finely chopped

1 teaspoon ginger paste

1 teaspoon garlic paste

1 teaspoon Sakahar Barha Masala (Vegetable Garam Masala, see page 194)

½ teaspoon ground turmeric

1 teaspoon ground cumin

1 teaspoon ground coriander

1 teaspoon Kashmiri chilli powder, or medium hot chilli powder

150g (5½oz) tomatoes, chopped

Salt, to taste

Rinse the beans under warm running water. Place them in a bowl, cover with 600ml (2½ cups) of water at room temperature and soak overnight, ideally in a warm place. The next day, drain the water. If the beans have started sprouting, you can cook them. If not, rinse them, cover with water and leave them to soak for another day or two. You can also wrap them in a wet muslin (cheesecloth) and leave to sprout for a couple of days.

Place the sprouted beans in a pressure cooker with 1litre (4 cups) of water and cook for 15–20 minutes, until soft. Alternatively, place the beans and 1 litre (4 cups) of water in a medium, heavy-based saucepan. Bring to the boil and simmer for 1–1½ hours, or until soft but not mushy.

Heat the ghee in a separate heavy-based saucepan. Add the jwanu and tejpaat leaves. When the seeds crackle, add the onion and sauté for 10–12 minutes, until golden brown. Add the ginger and garlic pastes and all the spices and stir-fry for 1 minute, until aromatic, but make sure they do not burn.

Add the chopped tomatoes, stir well, and cook for 5 minutes, or until soft. Pour the tempering into the beans. Simmer for 15–20 minutes. You want a thick consistency, between a soup and a stew.

Adjust the seasoning with salt and serve hot.

# Sandheko bhogate

*Pomelo & yogurt salad*

Pomelo, like citron and mandarin, are natives of Asia. All other citrus fruits are hybrids of these. A pomelo is sweeter than a grapefruit and makes an addictive snack when mixed with spices and yogurt, as here in this recipe.

We serve this snack during the Chhat Parva, a festival dedicated to the Sun God. We thank the God of light with food offerings and pray for longevity and prosperity. The festival takes place between August and November.

650g (23oz) bhogate, or pomelo, about 200g (7oz) of flesh

100g (½ cup) natural (plain) Greek yogurt

1 teaspoon caster (superfine) sugar

½ teaspoon salt

¼ teaspoon dried chilli flakes

2 teaspoons lemon juice

2 teaspoons mustard oil

### For the tempering

1 teaspoon mustard oil

½ teaspoon fenugreek seeds

½ teaspoon ground turmeric

¼ teaspoon Kashmiri chilli powder, or medium hot chilli powder

Prepare the bhogate (or pomelo). Remove the peel and white bitter membrane. Separate the flesh into small pieces.

Mix the bhogate (or pomelo) flesh with the yogurt, sugar and salt in a bowl and set aside.

For the tempering, heat the 1 teaspoon of mustard oil in a non-stick frying pan. Add the fenugreek seeds and cook until they darken. Add the turmeric and chilli powder. Cook over low heat for a few seconds, stirring all the time and making sure that the spices do not burn.

Add the tempering to the bhogate and yogurt mix along with the chilli flakes, lemon juice and the 2 teaspoons of mustard oil. Mix well, and adjust the seasoning adding more sugar, salt, chilli powder or lemon juice to taste. Leave to cool before serving.

# Pakku

*Dry festive goat meat*

The Dashain festival is our longest festival, celebrated for 10 days, around September and October. It is a time of joyous family reunion and food sharing. Pakku is one of the traditional dishes prepared during this festival. The meat, usually goat, is cooked with a generous amount of ghee, enough to completely cover the meat – this is a traditional method of preservation that would have allowed the dish to be kept for longer. You can prepare this recipe with lamb, buffalo or beef.

900g (2lb) goat or mutton, bone in, cut into 2.5-cm (1-in) pieces

5 tablespoons ghee (clarified butter)

3 tablespoons fresh coriander (cilantro), chopped, to garnish

**For the marinade**

5 tablespoons mustard oil

1 large red onion, finely chopped

1 teaspoon garlic paste

1 teaspoon ginger paste

½ teaspoon ground turmeric

1 teaspoon ground cumin

1 teaspoon ground coriander

1 teaspoon Kashmiri chilli powder, or medium hot chilli powder

1 teaspoon Mangsahaar Masala (Meat Garam Masala, see page 193)

1½ teaspoons salt

**To serve**

Bhat (Plain Rice, see page 169), or roti bread

Place all the ingredients for the marinade in a large bowl. Stir until well blended. Add the meat pieces and stir well, making sure the pieces are well coated with marinade. Place in the refrigerator and leave for at least 4–5 hours, or overnight.

Take the meat out of the refrigerator about 1 hour before cooking it.

Heat a couple of tablespoons of the ghee in a heavy-based pan. Add the meat and cook over medium heat for a couple of minutes, until the meat is well seared. Then simmer, covered, over very low heat, for 1½–2 hours. You want the meat to be tender and falling off the bone. Stir the meat occasionally, adding another tablespoon of the ghee each time, making sure the meat does not stick to the bottom of the pan.

Sprinkle with chopped coriander and serve hot with rice or roti bread.

# Selroti

*Fried ring bread*

Made of rice, ghee (clarified butter) and sugar, these sweet pretzel-like rings are one of the traditional offerings to the goddess Lakshmi during the Dashain festival in October and the Tihar festival in November. The breads are fried first thing in the morning. Some of the rings are reserved for offerings and the rest shared with family and friends. Popular in the hills and high mountains of the Himalayan region, a selroti recipe is a well-guarded secret, passed on from one generation to the next. Selroti are also cooked for wedding ceremonies. They should be eaten on the day they are made.

400g (generous 2¼ cups) basmati rice, preferably extra-long

1 teaspoon fenugreek seeds

150g (⅔ cup) ghee (clarified butter), melted

130g (scant ¾ cup) caster (superfine) sugar

2 tablespoons semolina

½ teaspoon baking powder

1 litre (4 cups) vegetable oil or ghee (clarified butter), for deep-frying

**To serve (optional)**

Aloo Ko Achar (Potato Pickle, see page 163)

Masala Chiya (Masala Tea, see page 209)

Bhang Ki Chutney (Hemp Seed Chutney, see page 156)

*A kitchen thermometer*

Place the rice and fenugreek seeds in a bowl. Cover with water and leave to soak overnight.

The next day, drain the rice mixture and wash under running water until the water becomes clear.

Place the rice and 100ml (scant ½ cup) of water in a food processor and process until you get a thick paste. Add a bit more water if the mixture is too thick. Transfer to a bowl and add the melted ghee, sugar, semolina and baking powder. Whisk until well blended, adding about 50ml (3½ tablespoons) more water. You want the consistency of a thin pancake batter. Leave to rest for 2–3 hours. When ready, check the consistency; if it has thickened, dilute it a bit.

Heat the vegetable oil or ghee in a medium wok or sauté pan until it reaches 250°C (500°F). It should be about 7.5cm (3in) deep. Fill a piping (pastry) bag with the mixture. Quickly pipe thin circles into the hot oil. The quicker you are, the rounder the shape will be. Cook for about 1 minute, then lift the ring with the end of a chopstick and flip it to cook the other side for another minute. It should be golden and crisp. Make 1 selroti at a time.

Serve hot or at room temperature, ideally with any or all of the suggested accompaniments listed.

# Yomari

*Sweet rice-flour dumplings*

Yomari is the most iconic sweet in Nepal. It is a rice flour dumpling, prepared during the Yomari Punhi, the rice harvest festival celebrated in December after the first rice is harvested. The origin of this sweet is unclear and its fig-like shape is often described as a fish or a Buddhist temple gajur (the ornate top part of a temple).

This sweet is made as an offering to Annapurna, the goddess of grains to thank her for the harvest. Yomari is traditionally filled with Chaku, a molasses toffee mixed with dark sesame seeds. It is steamed and eaten warm. My take on Yomari, which was one of the *MasterChef* dishes I cooked, is filled with oozing chilli-flavoured chocolate and topped with the zesty kick of fresh orange and the warmth of cinnamon.

**For the dough**

150g (1 cup plus 2 tablespoons) rice flour

30g (¼ cup) cornflour (cornstarch)

½ teaspoon sugar

150ml (⅔ cup) boiling water

**For the filling**

100g (3½oz) 55% dark chocolate

50g (2oz) 70% dark chocolate

⅛ teaspoon dried chilli flakes

3 tablespoons milk powder

1 tablespoon caster (superfine) sugar

**To serve (optional)**

Fresh orange segments

Ground cinnamon, to sprinkle

*A steamer basket*

~

To make the rice dumplings, mix the flours and sugar in a bowl. Add the boiling water, and start mixing with a wooden spatula, then with your hand. The dough will be very hot but it needs to be mixed and kneaded while hot. If it is too hot, you can wear a kitchen glove. Continue mixing until a dough is formed.

Transfer the dough to a work surface. Using the heel of your hand, press and stretch the dough away from you, fold it back together and press-stretch again for 6–8 minutes, until smooth and elastic. Wrap in a kitchen towel (dishcloth) and let it rest for 20–30 minutes, at room temperature. Meanwhile, prepare the filling. Finely grate both chocolates (or cut into chunks and reduce to a powder in a food processor or blender).

Transfer the grated chocolates to a small saucepan. Add the rest of the filling ingredients and mix well. Place the saucepan over low heat for a few seconds to slightly melt the chocolate and combine the mixture into a thick paste, not a runny mixture. Divide the paste into 12 even spoonfuls (about 15g (½oz) each and shape each one into a 5cm (2-in) cone.

Divide the rice dough into 12 pieces, about 25g (1oz) each. Shape each piece into a ball and using your fingers, flatten each ball into a thin disc. Place a cone of chocolate in the centre and shape the disc around into a large cone. Pull a bit of dough on one side to make a pointy end and shape the top of the cone into two horns. Repeat with the rest of the dough.

Place the yomari in a steamer basket and steam in batches for 8–10 minutes until translucent. Keep them covered and enjoy them warm, with fresh orange segments and with a little cinnamon sprinkled over the top, if you like.

They are best eaten when freshly made.

# Pickles, Chutneys & Side Salads

The word we use for condiments is achar. The variety of achar recipes in Nepal can easily compete with the number of our festivals and could be the subject of a separate book! Just the word achar is a story in itself...

People's definition of achar differs depending on where they live and what their background is. Certain ethnic groups have their own achar recipes, in the same way a family would also have its own recipe passed down from one generation to the next. We even have a specific term for achar made to last several months: purano achar. As a general rule, achar with a smooth consistency are chutneys and chunky achar are pickles. Then again, this rule may differ according to regions or communities. We also classify side salads as achar. This is why Gundruk Ra Bahtmas (Fermented Greens & Soybean Salad, see page 161) and Aloo Ko Achar (Potato Pickle, see page 163) are both included in this chapter.

Our condiments serve many purposes. Their main one is the preservation of ingredients but achar also bring nutritious balance to a meal using herbs, spices and seeds. Chilli and vinegar are not just there to preserve the food, they also stimulate our appetites and aid digestion. But my love of pickles and chutneys mainly rests on flavour, and how they elevate a simple meal of rice and dal with tanginess, sweetness and pungency.

Karela Ko Chutney (Bitter Gourd Chutney, see page 147) is the perfect example of how one preparation can have the perfect balance of bitter, salty, sweet and sour. Bhang Ki Chutney (Hemp Seed Chutney, see page 156), was a big hit when I served it on *MasterChef*. Food writer and critic Tom Parker Bowles loved "its sharpness and green vibrancy". For me, nothing wakes up your tastebuds like achar.

---

## "Our condiments serve many purposes. Their main one is the preservation of ingredients but achar also bring nutritious balance to a meal using herbs, spices and seeds."

---

The variety of achar we produce in Nepal is endless because they can be prepared from such a wide range of ingredients: fruits, vegetables, seeds or even dried fish. The consistency is important. Some achar have a loose consistency similar to a sauce, like the delicious Til Ko Golbheda Ko Achar (Tomato Sesame Chutney, see page 151) which is served with my Steamed Chicken Momos on page 43. We like our dumplings served with a sauce, but we prefer to dip our breads in a thicker or chunkier achar. Some of our achar can even be powdery, like Alas Ko Dhulo Achar (Flaxseed Chutney, see page 149), which is simply a mixture of flaxseeds and spices, reduced to a powder and seasoned with lemon juice.

I use an electric spice grinder in many of my recipes for convenience, but when it comes to chutney, I prefer the traditional method of grinding with a pestle and mortar (khal), because it is easier to control the consistency.

My favourite one to use consists of a flat stone as a mortar and a cylinder stone, similar to a rolling pin, as a pestle. I find rolling easier than pounding when you need to reduce seeds or spices to a powder. Dry roasting is a taste enhancer. Dry roast spices until they start to release their aroma, and seeds until they turn golden or a shade darker.

We often cook over a wood fire in Nepal which gives any ingredient a smoky taste. We use it like an extra spice. In a few of these chutneys, I like to roast chillies and tomatoes over fire. You can achieve the same result using a barbecue, or for small ingredients like chillies, the flame of a gas hob (stovetop). All my condiments are healthy and nutritious. Some can be prepared in advance and kept for a few weeks, while others are best enjoyed straight away for their piquant freshness.

*Following pages:* A tea shop in Bupsa, a small Sherpa village in the Solukhumbu district of Nepal.

*Right:* Gundruk, an ingredient made by fermenting and drying leafy greens.

*Below:* Two pin badges, one depicting the cross kukri, the unique and distinct symbol of the Gurkha regiment, and the other, the Nepali flag.

*Bottom:* Women selling mangoes and other fruits in Bhaktapur, Kathmandu.

# Karela ko chutney

*Bitter gourd chutney*

In this chutney recipe, I play with the intense bitterness of Karela (bitter gourd, see page 13), by balancing it with salty, sweet, sour and spicy flavours. Make sure you check that balance has been achieved, and adjust it at the end if needed.

I like to serve this with the Aloo Chop Sag Wala (Spiced Spinach, Fig & Potato Croquettes, see page 30), but you can also enjoy it simply with roti bread.

250g (9oz) karela (bitter gourd)

2 tablespoons vegetable oil

2 garlic cloves, chopped

30g (1oz) fresh ginger, peeled and chopped

4 fresh green chillies, tailed and chopped

½ teaspoon salt, to taste

100g (¾ cup) raisins or sultanas (golden raisins)

¼ teaspoon ground turmeric

75ml (⅓ cup) store-bought tamarind paste, or make your own (see page 15)

1 tablespoon fresh coriander (cilantro), chopped

Juice of 1 lime

25g (⅛ cup) store-bought fried chana dal snack

*An airtight container, for storing*

Cut the karela in half lengthways. Using a teaspoon, scrape out the seeds and soft white part from the centre and discard. Finely slice the hollowed shells.

Heat the oil in a non-stick frying pan. Add the garlic, ginger and chillies and cook for a couple of minutes over medium heat. Add the sliced karela and salt. Cook for 5 minutes, or until soft. The salt will help break the fibres of the karela. Add the raisins or sultanas and cook for 1–2 minutes, until puffed up. Remove from the heat and leave to cool.

Place the cooled mixture in a blender (or use a stick blender). Add the rest of the ingredients and blend to a fine paste. Add a little water if needed. Check the seasoning and adjust to taste, adding salt, raisins or sultanas, tamarind paste or lime juice, as needed.

Stored in an airtight container and refrigerated, this will keep for up to 1 week.

# Badam ko chutney

*Coriander & peanut chutney*

The freshness of this chutney is perfect to accompany Sherpa Roti (Sherpa Fried Bread, see page 180) and Pyaj Ke Kachari (Crispy Onion Beignets, see page 39). To keep the colour a vibrant green, prepare it at the last minute.

150g (5½oz) fresh coriander (cilantro)

50g (⅓ cup) blanched peanuts

15g (½oz) fresh ginger, peeled and chopped

3 garlic cloves, chopped

3 green chillies, tailed and chopped

75ml (⅓ cup) vegetable oil

1 teaspoon lemon juice

1 tablespoon caster (superfine) sugar

1 teaspoon salt

*An airtight container, for storing*

Wash the coriander and pat dry with kitchen paper (paper towels). Chop roughly.

Combine all the ingredients in a large pestle and mortar and crush to obtain a thick paste. Alternatively, blend all the ingredients in a small food processor.

Taste and adjust the seasoning, adding more sugar, salt or lemon juice as needed.

This should be eaten on the day it is made, and stored in an airtight container until ready to serve.

# Alas ko achar

*Flaxseed chutney*

Flaxseeds grow well in the temperate climate of the Himalayan hills. To get the full nutritional value of these super seeds, they need to be crushed. If your blender is not powerful enough, grind the seeds in an electric spice grinder or coffee grinder, then mix with the other ingredients. This is a dry powder style chutney seasoned with lemon juice. We serve it on the side along with other chutneys. We also dip our freshly fried breads into it.

100g (¾ cup) flaxseeds

½ teaspoon cumin seeds

4 dried red chillies

¾ teaspoon salt

2½ tablespoons lemon juice

*A sterilized screwtop jar, for storing*

Toast the flaxseeds in a non-stick frying pan over medium heat. When they release their aroma and start to puff up, transfer to a plate, spread them out and leave to cool.

In the same frying pan, dry roast the cumin seeds and chillies until they are slightly charred. Remove from the pan, set aside and leave to cool.

Combine the toasted seeds and chillies in an electric spice blender and process until you get a powder. Season with the salt and stir in the lemon juice.

Stored in a sterilized screwtop jar and refrigerated, this will keep for up to 2 months.

# Til ra hariyo kursani ko achar

*Sesame & green chilli pickle*

Sesame seeds are an important part of Nepali culture, both for religious offerings and in our healthy diet. They bring creaminess to this pickle and balance the heat of the chillies.

12 fresh green chillies, tailed and slit lengthways

100g (¾ cup) white sesame seeds

3 tablespoons mustard oil

½ teaspoon fenugreek seeds

2 timmur peppercorns, or Sichuan peppercorns

1 teaspoon ground turmeric

Juice of 2 limes

½ tablespoon fresh coriander (cilantro), chopped

½ teaspoon salt

*An airtight container, for storing*

Char the green chillies over the low embers of a barbecue (outdoor grill), or pierce them with a fork and rotate over an open gas flame on the hob (stovetop) until the skin is evenly blackened. Set aside and leave to cool.

Toast the sesame seeds in a non-stick frying pan over medium heat until golden. Set aside and leave to cool. In a pestle and mortar, or an electric spice grinder, crush the sesame seeds to a paste with 75ml (⅓ cup) of water.

Heat the mustard oil in the same frying pan until hot and a light shimmer appears on the surface. Add the fenugreek seeds. When the fenugreek seeds turn golden brown, add the charred chillies and fry for 30 seconds. Add the timmur and turmeric and stir for a few seconds, being careful not to let them burn. Remove the pan from the heat and add the sesame paste, lime juice and coriander. Season with the salt and leave to cool.

Stored in an airtight container and refrigerated, this will keep for up to 1 week.

# Til ko golbheda ko achar

*Tomato sesame chutney*

Traditionally, momos (see page 43) are served with a spicy sweet and sour tomato chutney. Mine has sesame seeds for texture and timmur (see page 17) for extra tang.

3 tablespoons white sesame seeds

2 tablespoons vegetable oil or mustard oil

½ teaspoon cumin seeds

¼ teaspoon timmur, or Sichuan peppercorns, lightly crushed

15g (½oz) fresh ginger, peeled and finely chopped

3 garlic cloves, finely chopped

3 dried red chillies, tailed and each cut into 3–4 pieces

1 teaspoon Kashmiri chilli powder, or medium hot chilli powder

½ teaspoon Nepali Barha Masala (Nepali Garam Masala, see page 190)

½ teaspoon ground turmeric

500g (18oz) tomatoes, chopped

½ teaspoon salt

1 tablespoon lemon, or lime juice

15g (½oz) fresh coriander (cilantro), chopped

*An airtight container, for storing*

Heat a non-stick frying pan over medium heat. Toast the sesame seeds for 6–7 minutes, until golden brown. Transfer to a plate and set aside to cool. Roughly blend the seeds in an electric spice grinder. You want to retain some texture.

Heat the oil in a separate non-stick frying pan over medium heat. Add the cumin seeds and cook until they crackle. Add the timmur, ginger, garlic and chillies and cook for 5 minutes, until soft.

Combine all the ground spices in a small bowl. Add 1 tablespoon of water and mix into a paste. Add this to the pan and fry for another minute or so, stirring all the time.

Add the chopped tomatoes and salt, and cook until the tomatoes soften and turn into a mash.

Combine the tomato mixture, the roughly blended sesame seeds, lemon or lime juice and coriander. Blend until smooth. Adjust the seasoning, adding more lemon or lime juice, or salt if needed.

Stored in an airtight container and refrigerated, this will keep for up to 1 week.

# Hariyo khursani ko achar

*Green chilli pickle*

Here, the chillies are simply dipped in vinegar and coated in mustard. Quick and easy, this is a very spicy pickle, when you need that extra chilli kick. They are part of the achar selection that we enjoy with almost every meal. Serve to accompany a meal, or with bread and rice.

16 small fresh green bird's eye green chillies

50ml (3½ tablespoons) white wine vinegar

2 tablespoons store-bought wholegrain mustard

*A sterilized screwtop jar, for storing*

Tail and slit the chillies in half lengthways. If you want a milder pickle, scrape out the seeds, if not, leave them in. Pour the vinegar into a shallow, non-metal container.

Dip each chilli half in the vinegar, then fill and coat with mustard. Place in the sterilized jar, seal and leave at room temperature for at least 24 hours to ferment.

Stored in the jar and refrigerated, this will keep for up to 2 weeks.

# Tama ko achar

*Bamboo shoot pickle*

Tama is one of our most popular fermented vegetables (see page 15). Harvested in the summer, the young bamboo shoots are fermented and consumed throughout the year. Behind the sourness you can really taste the freshness of the bamboo shoots. Added at the end of cooking, they will add a special tang to soups and curries. I like to use them as a pickle to accompany dal and rice.

This particular recipe is easy and quick to make. The bamboo shoots are simply crushed, then mixed with a spicy, mustard oil tempering.

200g (7oz) tama (fermented bamboo shoots), rinsed and dried

½ teaspoon salt

2 tablespoons mustard oil

½ teaspoon mustard seeds

¼ teaspoon ground turmeric

½ teaspoon Kashmiri chilli powder, or medium hot chilli powder

½ tablespoon freshly squeezed lemon juice

*A sterilized screwtop jar, for storing*

Roughly chop the tama. Place in a pestle and mortar with the salt and crush to reduce into a rough paste with a chunky texture. Transfer to a bowl.

Heat the mustard oil in a small non-stick frying pan over high heat. When the oil is hot, add the mustard seeds. When they crackle, add the turmeric and chilli powder and immediately remove from the heat, being careful that the ground spices do not burn. Pour over the crushed tama. Stir until well blended.

Mix in the lemon juice, adjust the seasoning, adding more salt or lemon juice if needed.

Stored in a sterilized screwtop jar and refrigerated, this will keep for up to 2 weeks.

# Hariyo aap ra nariyal ko achar

*Green mango & coconut chutney*

Green mangoes are perfect for chutneys as they add just the right level of sourness. You can get frozen grated coconut in Asian food stores. It is as good as a fresh coconut without the complication of cracking and grating.

4 small green mangoes

½ teaspoon salt

1 teaspoon Kashmiri chilli powder, or medium hot chilli powder

4 garlic cloves, chopped

15g (½oz) fresh ginger, peeled and chopped

50g (¾ cup) grated fresh or frozen coconut

1 tablespoon caster (superfine) sugar

1 tablespoon lemon juice

1 tablespoon fresh coriander (cilantro) leaves

2 tablespoons vegetable oil

*An airtight container, for storing*

Peel and stone the mangoes and cut the flesh into small dice. Crush the mango pieces and salt in a large pestle and mortar to break them up. Add the rest of the ingredients and crush into a paste. Alternatively, place the mango pieces and salt in a food processor and pulse a few times, until slightly crushed.

Add the rest of the ingredients and process to a coarse paste.

Check and adjust the seasoning, adding more salt, sugar or lemon juice, to taste.

Stored in an airtight container and refrigerated, this will keep for 3–4 days.

# Bhang ki chutney

*Hemp seed chutney*

Hemp grows wild in the Terai, very often on the side of the roads. We pick the seeds when they start to dry on the plant and continue the drying process at home. They are then roasted, crushed and only the tender seeds are used for chutneys.

The link between cooking and nutrition is important for us. Hemp seeds are one of the best plant proteins, packed with amino acids. It is the perfect accompaniment to Selroti (Fried Ring Bread, see page 137), Sherpa Roti (Sherpa Fried Bread, see page 180) and Aloo Chop Sag Wala (Spiced Spinach & Fig Potato Croquettes, see page 30).

100g (1 cup) hulled hemp seeds

3 wild garlic leaves, or 1 large garlic clove, chopped

15g (½oz) fresh ginger, peeled and chopped

2 fresh green chillies, tailed and chopped

100g (3½oz) fresh coriander (cilantro)

2 tablespoons lemon juice

3 tablespoons vegetable oil

¾ teaspoon salt

*An airtight container, for storing*

Dry roast the hemp seeds in a non-stick frying pan over medium heat for about 5 minutes, or until they reach a light golden colour. Place in a bowl and leave to cool.

In the same frying pan, dry roast the wild garlic leaves (or chopped garlic clove), ginger and chillies without oil for a few minutes, until dry and lightly charred. Place in a bowl and leave to cool.

Wash the coriander under running water. Shake to remove most of the water but keep it wet. You will need the moisture to loosen the consistency of the chutney.

Place the toasted seeds, wild garlic leaves (or chopped garlic) and ginger in a large pestle and mortar. Add the rest of the ingredients and crush into a paste. Alternatively, place all the ingredients in a food processor and blend into a loose, chunky paste. Add a bit more water if needed. Adjust the seasoning, adding more salt or lemon juice if needed and leave to cool.

Stored in an airtight container and refrigerated, this will keep for 4–5 days.

# Tamatar ko guliyo achar

*Sweet tomato chutney*

Gud – sometimes also spelt gur – is another name for jaggery. Golden in colour, this unrefined sugar can easily be found in Asian food stores. It is produced by boiling down the juice of crushed sugar cane without filtering out the molasses. It is that taste of molasses, combined with hot chillies, that gives this tomato chutney its wonderfully complex flavour.

Serve with fried bread or to accompany a main dish.

2 tablespoons vegetable oil

½ teaspoon cumin seeds

¼ teaspoon fennel seeds

1 tejpaat (Nepali bay leaf)

2 dried hot red chillies

600g (20oz) tomatoes, deseeded and chopped

1¼ teaspoons Kashmiri chilli powder, or medium hot chilli powder

1 tablespoon raisins

100g (½ cup) gud (jaggery)

Salt, to taste

*A sterilized screwtop jar, for storing*

Heat the oil in a non-stick frying pan over medium heat. Add the cumin seeds and fennel seeds, tejpaat and dried red chillies. When the seeds start to crackle, add the chopped tomato flesh and cook for 5–10 minutes, or until it softens.

Add the chilli powder, raisins and gud. Simmer for 15 minutes, uncovered, or until the liquid has almost reduced, the mixture thickens and the chutney turns glossy. Leave to cool and season to taste with salt.

Stored in a sterilized screwtop jar and refrigerated, this will keep for up to 2 weeks.

# Hariyo tamatar ko achar

*Green tomato chutney*

Smokiness is an important taste in this chutney. For this, the green tomatoes are slowly charred over the low embers of a fire but a gas flame will do the trick.

300g (10½oz) green tomatoes

25g (1oz) fresh green chillies

6 garlic cloves, finely chopped

30g (1oz) fresh ginger, peeled and chopped

A small handful of fresh coriander (cilantro)

2 tablespoons mustard oil

¼ teaspoon sugar

1 teaspoon salt

*An airtight container, for storing*

Char the green tomatoes over the low embers of a barbecue (outdoor grill), or pierce them with a fork and rotate over an open gas flame on the hob (stovetop) until the skin is evenly blackened. Leave to cool, then remove the skin and chop the flesh. Slightly char the chillies in the same way and chop.

Combine the chopped tomato flesh, chopped chillies and the rest of the ingredients in a large pestle and mortar. Crush to obtain a thick paste.

Stored in an airtight container and refrigerated, this will keep for 2–3 days.

# Titiri ko achar

*Tamarind chutney*

Everyone has their own variation on a tamarind chutney recipe. Mine is sour, sweet, hot and peppery. It will add just the right tang to any snack.

~

150ml (²/₃ cup) store-bought tamarind paste, or homemade tamarind paste (see page 15)

1 tejpaat (Nepali bay leaf)

1 small cinnamon stick, broken into shards

1 black cardamom, lightly crushed

150g (¾ cup) gud (jaggery), chopped into small pieces

¾ teaspoon Kashmiri chilli powder, or medium hot chilli powder

1½ teaspoons ground ginger

1 teaspoon black peppercorns, lightly crushed

¼ teaspoon salt

A pinch of bire noon (Himalayan black salt, see page 12)

*A sterilized screwtop jar, for storing*

Place all the ingredients in a heavy-based pan with 500ml (2 cups) of water. Bring to a simmer over medium heat, stirring from time to time, making sure the gud is completely dissolved. Continue simmering, uncovered, on very low heat for 30–40 minutes, or until you have a thick syrupy consistency.

Pass through a fine sieve (strainer) and leave to cool.

Stored in a sterilized screwtop jar and refrigerated, this will keep for up to 1 month.

---

# Pyaj ko achar

*Red onion & chilli salad*

This is a side salad that can be served with every meal, along with a few chutneys. It goes well with my Poleko Machha Ra Jhol (Spiced Monkfish with Sesame & Tomato Sauce, see page 79).

1 red onion, cut into thin wedges

¼ teaspoon Kashmiri chilli powder, or medium hot chilli powder

1 teaspoon lemon juice

¼ teaspoon salt

1 teaspoon chopped fresh coriander (cilantro)

Place all the ingredients except the coriander in a bowl.

Mix with your fingers for a couple of minutes. The lemon and salt will draw some moisture out of the onion.

When the mixture is moist, mix in the coriander and serve immediately.

# Gundruk ra bhatmas

*Fermented greens & soybean salad*

Gundruk is made by fermenting and drying leafy greens (see page 12). The fermentation process preserves the vitamins and minerals, making it an incredibly nutritious storecupboard ingredient. Gundruk is mainly used in soups, but I find that its sour taste suits this slightly pickle-like salad, which can be served to accompany any meal.

50–70g (1¾–2½ oz) gundruk (dried fermented greens)

**For the fried soybeans**

250 ml (1 cup) vegetable oil

50g (⅓ cup) dried soybeans

**For the dressing**

3 tomatoes

1 teaspoon mustard oil

½ teaspoon cumin seeds

2 dried red chillies, crushed

¼ teaspoon ground turmeric

½ teaspoon salt

1 tablespoon lemon juice

⅛ teaspoon Timmur Ko Chhop (Timmur Spice Mix, see page 189)

1 tablespoon chopped fresh coriander (cilantro)

Soak the gundruk in a bowl of warm water for at least 30 minutes, or until well softened. Drain and squeeze between your hands to remove any excess water. Finely chop and set aside in a bowl.

To cook the fried soybeans, heat the oil in a small, non-stick frying pan until it reaches 170°C (340°F). Fry the soybeans for 4–5 minutes, until golden and puffed. Drain on kitchen paper (paper towels) and leave to cool. Using a pestle and mortar, roughly crush the soybeans into small pieces. Set aside.

Char the tomatoes over the low embers of a barbecue (outdoor grill), or pierce them with a fork and rotate over an open gas flame on the hob (stovetop) until the skin is evenly blackened. Leave to cool, then remove the skin, chop the flesh and transfer to a large pestle and mortar (or a food processor).

Heat the mustard oil in a small non-stick frying pan. Add the cumin seeds and chillies. When they crackle, remove from the heat, stir in the turmeric then immediately pour on top of the tomatoes into the pestle and mortar (or the food processor). Add the rest of the dressing ingredients and crush (or pulse if you are using a food processor) to obtain a thick paste. Adjust the seasoning, adding more salt or lemon if needed. Add this paste to the gundruk along with the crushed soybeans and mix well.

Serve at room temperature, or cold, on the day it is made.

# Aloo ko achar

*Potato pickle*

Between a potato salad and a pickle, this is a most addictive dish. The mustard oil and fenugreek are crucial ingredients here as they get absorbed into the warm potatoes, giving them a real pungent flavour.

I like to serve this as an accompaniment to monkfish, but it could also be simply served with Selroti (Fried Ring Bread, see page 137), rice, or dungri papad, a crispy, deep-fried snack.

500g (18oz) Red Bliss potatoes, or other waxy potatoes, peeled and diced

1 tablespoon white sesame seeds

50g (3 ½ tablespoons) salted butter, at room temperature

1 small red onion, finely chopped

⅓ cucumber, diced

3 fresh green chillies, finely chopped

1 tablespoon fresh coriander (cilantro), chopped

Juice of 1 lime

Salt, to taste

### For the tempering

60ml (¼ cup) mustard oil

1 teaspoon fenugreek seeds

35g (1 ¼oz) piece of fresh ginger, peeled and finely chopped

2 garlic cloves, finely chopped

50g (1 ¾oz) store-bought Indian mixed pickle from a jar

½ teaspoon ground turmeric

### To serve

Store-bought dungri papad

Boil the diced potatoes in a large pan of salted water for 15–20 minutes. Drain and place in a mixing bowl. Roughly crush them with a fork, cover to keep warm and set aside.

Dry roast the sesame seeds in a non-stick frying pan, until golden all over. Remove from the pan, set aside and leave to cool. Place in a pestle and mortar and crush to a powder. Alternatively, use an electric spice or coffee grinder.

Make the tempering. Heat the mustard oil in a large non-stick frying pan until hot and a slight shimmer appears on the surface. Add the fenugreek seeds and let them darken. Add the ginger and garlic and sauté for 1–2 minutes over high heat. Add the turmeric, and immediately remove the pan from the heat, otherwise the turmeric will burn.

Now add the potatoes and butter. When the butter has melted, add the sesame seed powder and rest of the ingredients to the pan and mix until well blended, being careful not to turn the mixture into a mash. You want to retain a chunky texture, Adjust the seasoning with extra lime juice and salt if needed.

Serve warm, or cold, on the day it is made.

# Grains & Breads

For us, rice is more than a grain, it is a social status and a religious offering. Favoured by the Rana rulers, it was the grain that only officials and landowners could afford and over time, rice has kept its rank of superior grain. Millet, barley and maize, grown in the hills and mountains were frowned upon despite a higher nutritional value.

Rice is eaten in many forms. Boiled, of course, but also pounded and flattened as flakes that we call chiura (see below). Every year, at the end of June or the beginning of July, depending on the monthly cycles of the moon, we celebrate the beginning of Ropain, the rice planting season. A hard but playful day of planting rice. This "Paddy Day" has become a national holiday. It corresponds with the start of the monsoon, when the paddy fields begin filling with water. Family and friends meet up to plant rice seedlings, sing and play knee-high in the mud. At the end of that day, covered in mud but happy, people share Dahi-chiura, a mix of yogurt, beaten rice and fruit, washed down with homemade brew.

Chiura is made with young rice. It is parboiled, roasted and then traditionally pounded in a giant pestle and mortar. This process is disappearing, and the flattening is now mechanized. Chiura keeps longer than rice. We eat the flakes in different ways. They can be dry-toasted, fried in oil or simply as they come out of the packet. They are perfect served with saucier curries to absorb all the delicious juices. You will find a recipe for toasted chiura with the Tama Ra Bungur Ko Masu (Pork & Bamboo Shoot Curry, see page 56).

We are also fond of puffed rice called bhuja (see page 14). The grains are toasted over high heat being constantly stirred until they puff up. They can be part of a recipe like in our Chana Chatpate (Crispy Potato & Puffed Rice Salad, see page 34) or as an accompaniment to snacks.

## "Family and friends meet up to plant rice seedlings, sing and play knee-high in the mud."

Of all the grains well-suited for the harsh climate of the Himalayas, millet is the one cultivated at the highest altitude, as high as 3500m (11,500ft), and which requires very little water. Millet is a gluten-free, high-protein cereal rich in vitamins and minerals. It is often eaten as a form of porridge, simply cooked with water and salt, and served with vegetables and dal. I like to cook millet as Kaguna Ko Pulao (Yellow Millet Pulao, see page 172) with added spices and nuts or dried fruits.

This chapter is also about bread (roti). Wheat is one of the important crops after rice and maize, and our breads are prepared with wheat flour and a variety of other flours and crushed grains, including rice, maize, millet and buckwheat. Each area and community has its own bread speciality. Like rice, they accompany each meal or are served with achar (see pages 142–143) for breakfast or as snacks. We rarely add yeast, preferring a natural and slow overnight fermentation, combined with the high heat of oil to give the breads their light, puffy texture. My favourite is Gwaramari (Newari Breakfast Bread, page 179), deep-fried little pillows of deliciousness that we eat in the Terai. I love watching the frying of these breads in the street food stalls; little mounds of sticky dough being dropped in concentric circles in cast-iron pans full of fizzing oil.

I have also included an easy recipe for Sherpa Roti (Sherpa Fried Bread, see page 180), the famous Himalayan bread. This Sherpa bread, Himalayan honey (read more about this on page 206) and Masala Chiya (Masala Tea, see page 209) make the perfect start to a hard day of labour in high altitude. Puri is another of our most popular fried breads. You will see puri served all over Nepal. It is also a favourite for family celebrations and festivals. The dough is rolled in thin rounds and, once in contact with hot oil, puffs up like a balloon. The result is a very crisp and light texture. Puri are most often served with Aloo Ko Tarkari (Potato Curry, see page 118), but also enjoyed with dal.

*Right:* A woman stands in a field of millet in the Pokhara Valley.

# Bhat

*Plain rice*

Rice is the most important food in our culture. We have two festivals to celebrate the beginning of the rice-planting season and its harvesting. We eat rice at every meal, and great care is put into cooking it.

Rice needs to be soaked to improve its fluffiness, but only for a short time or the grains will break while cooking. I have given an amount of water as a guideline, but every rice absorbs water differently. If you get used to a brand, you will soon know exactly how much water to use. Make sure to gently stir the rice once or twice during cooking to ensure that it cooks evenly.

250g (scant 1 ½ cups) basmati rice, preferably extra-long

¾ teaspoon salt

Rinse the rice 2 or 3 times, being careful not to break the grains. Leave to soak in tepid water for 25 minutes.

Drain the rice and place in a heavy-based saucepan fitted with a lid. Add 450ml (scant 2 cups) of water and the salt. Bring to the boil. Cover and cook over medium heat for 10 minutes. Stir gently once or twice, making sure the rice does not stick to the bottom.

When most of the water has been absorbed, and the rice and water are at the same level, reduce the heat to very low and cook, covered, for 10 minutes more. Turn off the heat and leave for a further 5 minutes. Gently fluff the rice and serve.

*Opposite:* Ghandruk village, set in the spectacular landscape of the Annapurna massif.

# Matter pulao

*Green pea pulao*

Pulaos are usually reserved for special occasions and festivals. At home, we simply have plain steamed rice (Bhat, see page 169). The secret of making pulao fluffy and light is to let the rice absorb most of the water, then finish cooking it in its own steam over very low heat.

450g (2½ cups) basmati rice, preferably extra-long, washed

5 tablespoons ghee (clarified butter)

1 teaspoon royal, or black cumin seeds

½ teaspoon cloves

1 teijpaat (Nepali bay leaf)

4 green cardamoms, lightly crushed

1 cinnamon stick

2 red onions, thinly sliced

2 teaspoons salt

150g (generous 1 cup) fresh, or frozen garden peas

A small handful of fresh mint leaves, shredded

A small handful of fresh coriander (cilantro) leaves, chopped

Soak the rice in tepid water for 25 minutes.

Meanwhile, heat the ghee in a large, heavy-based casserole pan fitted with a lid. Add the whole spices. When they crackle, add the sliced onions and 1 teaspoon of the salt. Cook over medium heat for 10–15 minutes until golden brown.

When the onions are ready, add the fresh or frozen peas and sauté for a couple of minutes. Add the rest of the salt and 800ml (3¼ cups) of water. Cover and bring to the boil.

Drain the rice from its soaking water and add to the aromatic boiling water. Cover and return to the boil. Simmer over medium heat for 10–15 minutes, stirring gently once or twice, making sure the rice doesn't stick to the bottom. When most of the water has been absorbed and the rice and water are at the same level, gently stir in the mint and coriander. Cover and leave over very low heat for 10 minutes.

Fluff the rice with a fork and serve hot with curry or dal.

# Kaguna ko pulao

*Yellow millet pulao*

Kodo (millet), grows particularly well in difficult terrain and climatic conditions. For this reason, it is widely grown in the hills and mountain regions where rice and wheat cannot be cultivated. It has other advantages: it keeps well and is highly nutritious. Millet comes in a variety of crops and is used for making porridge, bread and liquor. This pulao, made with a yellow kodo called kaguna, is my own creation.

This dish can be served as an accompaniment to Machha Ko Jhol (White Fish in Mustard & Onion Sauce, see page 80).

3 tablespoons vegetable oil

1 teaspoon cumin seeds

40g (1 ½oz) fresh ginger, peeled and chopped

3 garlic cloves, chopped

1 onion, finely chopped

1 teaspoon salt

3 fresh green chillies, tailed and chopped

250g (generous 1 ¼ cups) kaguna, or yellow millet, rinsed and drained

100g (½ cup) chopped canned, or fresh, tomatoes

1 ¾ teaspoons Nepali Barha Masala (Nepali Garam Masala, see page 190)

1 ¾ teaspoons ground coriander

1 ¾ teaspoons ground cumin

1 ½ teaspoons Kashmiri chilli powder, or medium hot chilli powder

50g (½ cup) chopped dried nuts, or dried fruits (optional)

3 tablespoons of fresh coriander (cilantro), chopped, plus extra leaves to garnish

50g (3 ½ tablespoons) unsalted butter, at room temperature

Heat the oil in a heavy-based non-stick saucepan over medium heat. Add the cumin seeds. When they start to crackle, add the chopped ginger and garlic, and cook for 1 minute. Add the onion, salt and green chillies. Cook for 3–4 minutes, until the onion softens.

Add the millet, stir well, and cook over low heat for 3–4 minutes, stirring occasionally to make sure nothing sticks at the bottom.

Stir in the canned or fresh tomatoes and ground spices. Cook for a couple of minutes, stirring occasionally. Add the dried nuts or fruits (if using) and 650ml (2¾ cups) of hot water. Stir well, then bring to a simmer.

Stir in the chopped coriander. Cover and cook over very low heat for 20–25 minutes, until all the liquid is absorbed and the millet is tender. Add a little more water if the mixture becomes too dry.

When the millet is ready, and just before serving, incorporate the butter, fluffing up the mixture with a fork.

Garnish with coriander leaves and serve hot.

# Terai bhuteko bhat

*Terai masala rice*

Rice is the most important crop in Nepal, most of it cultivated in the flat hills of the Terai. We have different names for rice whether it is uncooked (chaamal) or cooked (bhat). The crops vary in size, colour and shape. I prefer the long-grain rice, which is more fluffy and fragrant.

This vegetable and cashew pulao, typical of the Terai, is usually reserved for special occasions.

**For the rice**

250g (scant 1 ½ cups) basmati rice, preferably extra-long

1 ½ tablespoons ghee (clarified butter)

6 cardamoms, lightly crushed

6 cloves

50g (scant ½ cup) cashew nuts, roughly chopped

¾ teaspoon salt

**For the masala vegetables**

2 tablespoons ghee (clarified butter)

½ teaspoon cumin seeds

1 red onion, finely chopped

1 green (bell) pepper, diced

30g (¼ cup) diced carrots

30g (generous ¼ cup) diced cauliflower

50g (generous ⅓ cup) peeled and diced potato

½ teaspoon Sakahar Barha Masala (Vegetable Garam Masala, see page 194)

½ teaspoon ground coriander

½ teaspoon ground turmeric

1 tablespoon chopped fresh coriander (cilantro), chopped

**To serve (optional)**

Pickle or chutney of your choice

Natural (plain) yogurt

Rinse the rice 2 or 3 times, being careful not to break the grains. Leave to soak in tepid water for 25 minutes.

Heat the ghee in a heavy-based non-stick pan fitted with a lid. Add the cardamoms, cloves and cashew nuts, and cook for a couple of minutes, stirring often.

When the cashews are golden, add the rice and stir for a minute. Add 450ml (2 cups) of water and the salt, bring to the boil, cover and cook over medium heat for about 10 minutes. Stir gently once or twice, making sure the rice doesn't stick to the bottom. When most of the water has been absorbed and the rice and water are at the same level, reduce the heat to very low and cook, covered, for 10 minutes more.

Prepare the masala vegetables. Heat the ghee in a non-stick frying pan. When hot, add the cumin seeds. When they crackle, add the onion and sauté for 5 minutes until soft. Then add all the chopped vegetables and cook for 10–15 minutes, or until soft. Add the ground spices and cook for another minute, stirring occasionally.

Add the masala vegetables to the rice and gently mix until well incorporated, being careful not to break the rice grains.

Sprinkle with chopped coriander and serve hot, with any pickle or chutney and yogurt, if you like.

# Puri

*Fried puffed bread*

These little flat breads puff up like a balloon when cooked in hot oil. Their texture, wonderfully light and flaky, is unique. Achieving the right puffiness takes a bit of practice.

Our Aloo Ko Tarkari (Potato Curry) is so often eaten with puri, that I have included a method for making them with the curry recipe on page 118, so you can make then at the same time as the curry, if you like. But, as it is also served to accompany plenty of other curries and dals, such as the Chana Ko Dal (Spicy Chickpeas, see page 93), I feel that puri deserves its own place in this chapter.

500g (3¾ cups) plain (all-purpose) flour or roti (chapati) flour, or an equal mixture of both

2 teaspoons salt

1 tablespoon ghee (clarified butter) or vegetable oil, for working into the dough

1 litre (4 cups) vegetable oil, for deep-frying

2 tablespoons vegetable oil, for rolling

To make the puri dough. Combine the flour and salt into a bowl. Add the ghee, or oil, and, using your fingers, work the oil into the flour until well incorporated. Make a well in the flour and measure out 250ml (1 cup) of water. Add some of the water into the well and start mixing the dough, gradually adding the remaining water, a little at a time, until a firm dough forms.

Knead the dough well with your hands for about 10 minutes until soft and elastic.

Cover with a clean damp cloth and set aside for 15 minutes. Divide the dough into 20 pieces and keep them covered.

Heat the oil in a deep sauté pan until it reaches 190°C (375°F). Roll one of the dough pieces in your hand to make a smooth ball. Apply a little oil on the dough ball and roll it out on an oiled surface with a rolling pin to obtain a 10-cm (4-in) disc. Repeat with the other dough balls. Keep the discs covered with a wet cloth.

Place a puri in the hot oil. When it rises to the surface, press it down very gently into the oil with a skimmer. The puri will start puffing up. Flip it over and cook for a few seconds. When the puri are crisp and golden brown – this should take a couple of minutes on each side – remove from the oil and place on kitchen paper (paper towels) to drain.

Serve hot as an accompaniment to curries and dals.

# Gwaramari

*Newari breakfast fried bread*

These fried dumplings, served with chutney and Masala Chiya (Masala Tea, see page 209) is the traditional Newari breakfast. The dough, left to ferment overnight, will puff up in contact with the hot oil, producing a crisp fluffy dumpling. Be aware that the dough is extremely sticky, and you need to dip your fingers in a bowl of water before grasping some dough and dropping it into the hot oil. This is my take on gwaramari, with added spices.

You will need to start making these the day before you wish to eat them.

200g (1 ½ cups) maida flour, or plain (all-purpose) flour

¾ teaspoon salt

½ teaspoon finely ground or crushed black peppercorns

½ teaspoon ground turmeric

½ teaspoon ground cumin

½ teaspoon ground coriander

1 small garlic clove, chopped

1 teaspoon fresh ginger juice

1 ¼ teaspoons baking powder

200ml (scant 1 cup) water, at room temperature

about 500ml (2 cups) vegetable oil, for deep-frying

**To serve**

Chutney of your choice

*A kitchen thermometer*

In a mixing bowl, combine all the ingredients except the oil for deep-frying. Briefly whisk, until everything is just combined, then leave to rest in a warm place overnight. This will help relax the gluten and slightly ferment the dough, for a light, fluffy texture.

The next day, pour the oil into a heavy-based sauté pan. The oil should be about 3cm (1 ¼in) deep. Heat the oil until it reaches 170°C (340°F).

Mix the dough with your fingers for a couple of minutes. It should be sticky and stringy. Using wet fingers, carefully lift dollops of batter from the bowl and drop them into the hot oil. Fry for 30–60 seconds, then flip them over and cook for another 30–60 seconds. Lift the breads from the oil and drain on kitchen paper (paper towels). Repeat until you have used all of the batter.

Serve hot with chutney.

# Sherpa roti

*Sherpa fried bread*

With a soft and crispy crust, a sherpa fried bread is a simple irresistible treat. In the cold mornings of the Himalayas, they are the best way to start the day. Try it dipped in honey to accompany a cup of Masala Chiya (Masala Tea, see page 209), served with a pickle or chutney for a snack, or to accompany a meal.

Like any fried bread, it is best eaten when freshly made and still warm.

300g (2¼ cups) maida flour, or plain (all-purpose) flour

¼ teaspoon baking powder

1 teaspoon caster (superfine) sugar

½ teaspoon salt

1 egg

100ml (scant ½ cup) whole (full-fat) milk

1 litre (4 cups) vegetable oil, for deep-frying, plus extra for rolling

**To serve**

Honey, to drizzle (optional)

Tamatar Ko Guliyo Achar (Sweet Tomato Chutney, page 158)

Bhang Ki Chutney (Hemp Seed Chutney, page 156)

*A kitchen thermometer*

Place the flour, baking powder, sugar and salt in a bowl. Whisk with a fork until well blended.

Make a well in the centre of the flour. Crack the egg in the centre, then pour in half of the milk. Start mixing with your hand. Gradually add the rest of the milk and continue to mix until a soft dough forms.

Knead the dough for about 5 minutes until smooth and elastic. Cover and set aside for 2–3 hours.

Preheat the oven to 100°C (80°C fan/210°F/Gas ¼). Heat the oil in a deep saucepan until it reaches 180°C (350°F).

Meanwhile, divide the dough into 10 balls, about 45g (1½oz) each. Roll each ball in your hand until smooth and set aside on a plate. Cover with a kitchen towel (dishcloth).

Spread a little oil on your work surface. Using a rolling pin, roll a dough ball into a 15cm (6in) long oval shape, about 5mm (¼in) thick. With a sharp knife, or a pizza cutter, make 7 small cuts inside the dough; 3 parallel ones in the centre plus 2 at each end.

Place the dough into the hot oil and cook for 4–5 minutes on each side until puffed and golden brown. Keep warm in the low oven while you roll and cook the remaining dough balls.

Serve warm, drizzled with honey, if liked, and chutney.

# Spice Mixes & Garnishes

Spices play a huge role in Nepali cooking. You will find a short description of the typical – and some of the more unusual – ones we use in the Ingredients Directory (see pages 12–17), but I also want to highlight the importance of a few of them here.

If I had to choose which ingredients sum up the distinctive tastes found in Nepali cuisine, it would be timmur and mustard oil. Timmur (Nepali Sichuan peppercorns, see page 17) grows wild in the high plateaux of the Himalayas. It is botanically related to Sichuan peppercorn, but I find it to be more floral and perfumed in flavour. We actually use very little timmur in our dishes because it quickly becomes overpowering. In fact, one of the spice mixes we use is Timmur Ko Chhop (Timmur Spice Mix, see page 189), a recipe where we grind timmur with black peppercorns to soften its intensity and add that piquant note at the very end of cooking. The red timmur berries are harvested by hand, a difficult job because of the prickly nature of the bush. The berries are then spread out and left to dry in the sun. Even though timmur is abundant, the harvesting remains limited and artisanal.

When you buy mustard oil, make sure you get the best quality – many mustard oils are extracted with heat, or chemicals, or even diluted with palm oil. You want a supplier who guarantees traditional extraction, which is the only way the nutrients and the flavours remain in the oil. Pure mustard oil

is perfect for cooking because it has a high smoke point of about 250°C (480°F). It also has a delicious flavour so can be added to a salad or an achar (chutney or pickle) right at the end of the preparation.

You will discover through cooking the recipes in this book that balancing spices is an alchemy, one that is almost an art form. In this chapter, I have included five different recipes for Garam Masala Spice Mixes (see pages 190–194). There are three mixes that are each slightly tweaked to suit meat, chicken and vegetables, a go-to mix I simply call Nepali garam masala, and a whole-spice version of this. Each of these garam masala has its unique blend of spices that will give it its identity. For example, the Mangsahaar Masala (Meat Garam Masala, see page 193) has green cardamoms and jhhau (stone moss, see page 13), but these ingredients will not appear in the Sakahar Barha Masala (Vegetable Garam Masala, see page 194). Jhhau is a lichen found on tree barks in the hills of Eastern Nepal. It acts as a natural taste-enhancer, which gives this particular garam masala spice mix more intensity, so it is designed to be combined with the strong taste of meat.

My passion as a chef is to play with all these spices and constantly discover new ways to use them, or bring the most out of them. To repeat what I also say in the spice mix recipes themselves, do not buy or grind large amounts of whole spices in advance. If you are not using your ground spice mix regularly,

it is best to grind only what you need on the day you are cooking in order to to get the best flavour from your spices.

This chapter also contains a recipe for crisp garnishes, as Nepali cooking is not just about the balance of spices, it is also about creating contrasting and interesting textures. Lotus roots, okra and onion can all be slow fried to achieve maximum crispiness. You will find the recipe for these (Kurkure Kamal Kakdi, Kurkure Bhindi, Kurkure Pyaj) on page 198. They will not only add beautiful texture, but also zing, to many of your dishes.

> "You will discover through cooking my recipes that balancing spices is an alchemy, one that is almost an art form."

*Left:* A shopkeeper sits surrounded by his wares, with scales ready to sell spices by weight.

*Below left:* Chilli is milled by hand in a large mortar, with a rock being used as an effective pestle.

*Below right:* Jhhau (stone moss), timmur (Nepali Sichuan peppercorns) and gundruk (dried fermented greens) are all uniquely Nepali ingredients.

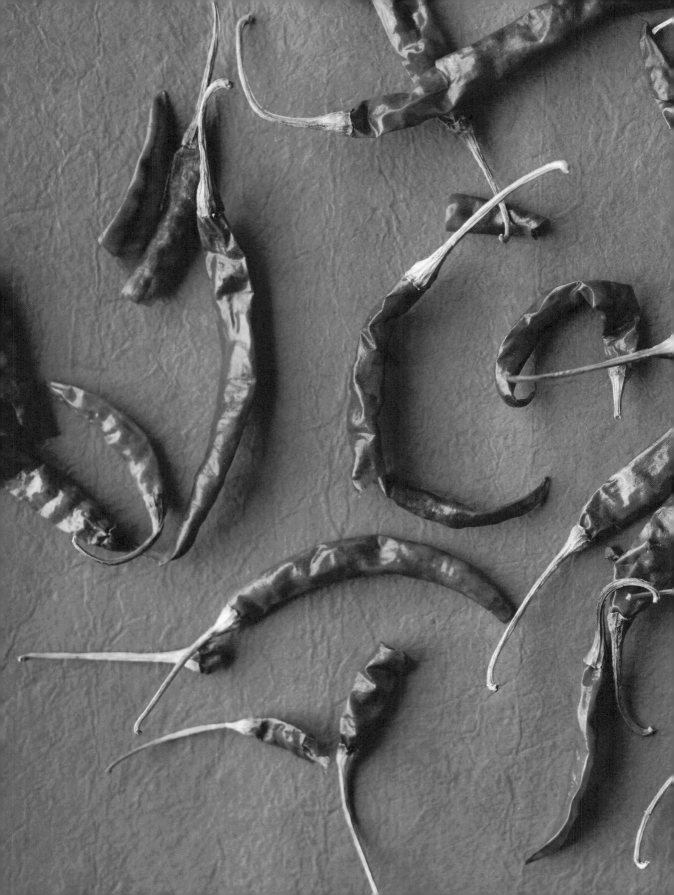

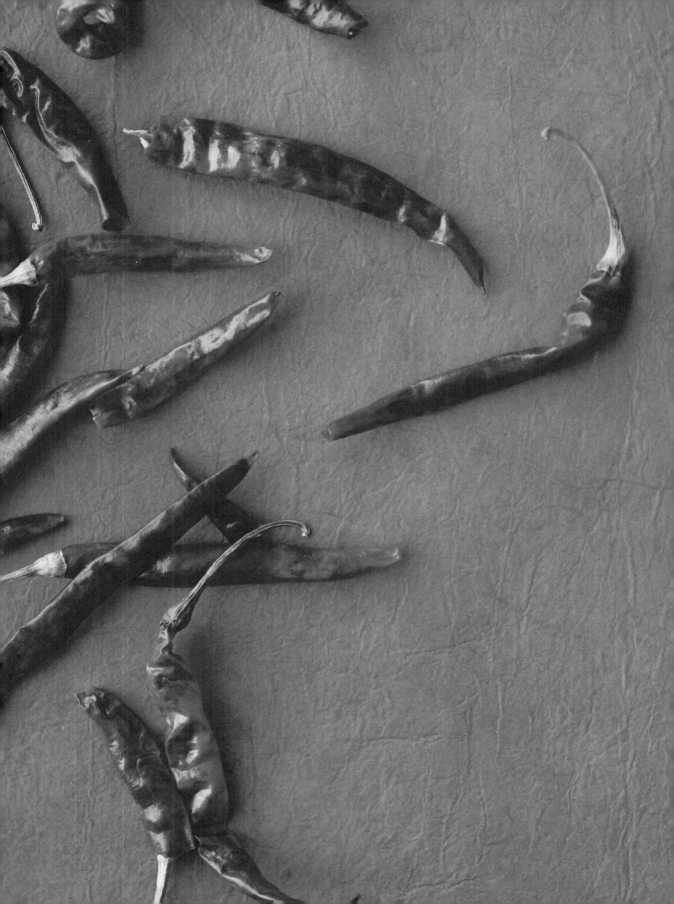

# Chatpate masala

*Chatpate spice mix*

This is the spice mix used in the Chana Chatpate (Crispy Potato & Puffed Rice Salad) on page 34. You will need to use extra-small, very hot dried red chillies for this.

6 small extra-hot dried red chillies, tailed

1 tablespoon coriander seeds

1 tablespoon mustard seeds

1 tablespoon cumin seeds

½ teaspoon timmur peppercorns, or Sichuan peppercorns

*A screw-top jar or airtight container, for storing*

Heat a non-stick frying pan over medium heat. Add all the spices and dry roast for 2–3 minutes, until they are fragrant, stirring often and making sure none of the spices burn. Reduce the heat if needed. Transfer to a plate and leave to cool.

Using a spice grinder or coffee grinder, grind the toasted and cooled whole spices until finely powdered.

Transfer to a screw-top jar or other airtight container. For best results, use this spice mix within 2 weeks.

# Timmur ko chhop

*Timmur spice mix*

Timmur is the Nepali Sichuan peppercorn (see page 17). Mixed with black peppercorns, I call it the magic spice. Use it to sprinkle on salads and snacks. This is a small enough quantity to make in a pestle and mortar.

2 tablespoons timmur peppercorns, or Sichuan peppercorns

¼ teaspoon black peppercorns

*A screw-top jar or airtight container, for storing*

Heat a non-stick frying pan over medium heat. Add the spices and dry roast for 2–3 minutes, until fragrant, stirring often and making sure none of the spices burn. Reduce the heat if needed. Transfer to a plate and leave to cool.

Reduce to a powder in a pestle and mortar, spice grinder or coffee grinder.

Transfer to a screw-top jar or other airtight container. For best results, use this spice mix within 2 weeks.

# Garam masala

Garam masala is what distinguishes one curry dish from another. My garam masala mixes have slight variations depending on whether I am cooking chicken, meat or vegetables. Garam masala should be added at the end of the cooking process, when it will release just the right amount of flavour. If it is added too early, it will mostly disappear and only the bitterness of the spices will remain.

Most of the spices I use are easy to find in Asian food shops. Only timmur (Nepali Sichuan peppercorn, see page 17) and jhhau (stone moss, see page 13) are specifically Nepali and need to be sourced in Nepali grocery shops or from specialist online retailers.

I can never stress enough the importance of using freshly ground spices. Whole spices will keep for six months – freshly ground spices will lose fifty per cent of their potency after just two weeks.

MAKES ABOUT 8 TABLESPOONS

## Nepali barha masala

*Nepali garam masala*

**For the whole spices**

2 teaspoons cumin seeds

2 tablespoons coriander seeds

1 teaspoon timmur peppercorns, or Sichuan peppercorns

1 teaspoon cloves

2 teaspoons black peppercorns

4 black cardamoms

2 teaspoons green cardamoms

5 tejpaat (Nepali bay leaves), crushed

7-cm (2¾-in) cinnamon stick, broken into shards

2 tablespoons jhhau (stone moss), optional

**For the ground spices**

1 tablespoon ground ginger

1 tablespoon freshly grated nutmeg (about ¾ of a whole nutmeg)

*A screw-top jar or airtight container, for storing*

Heat a non-stick frying pan. Add all the whole spices and dry roast over medium heat until they colour, puff up and start releasing their aroma. Transfer to a plate and leave to cool.

Using a spice grinder or coffee grinder, grind the toasted and cooled whole spices in batches until finely powdered. Mix in the ground spices until well blended.

Transfer to a screw-top jar or other airtight container. For best results, use this spice mix within 2 weeks.

# Luiche masala

*Chicken garam masala*

### For the whole spices

1 tablespoon dried garlic flakes

2 teaspoons cumin seeds

2 tablespoons coriander seeds

1 teaspoon timmur peppercorns,
   or Sichuan peppercorns

5 dried red chillies, crushed

2 teaspoons black peppercorns

2 teaspoons green cardamoms

1 teaspoon black mustard seeds

7-cm (2¾-in) cinnamon stick,
   broken into shards

### For the ground spices

1 tablespoon ground ginger

1 tablespoon freshly grated nutmeg
   (about ¾ of a whole nutmeg)

1 teaspoon ground turmeric

*A screw-top jar or airtight container,
   for storing*

To make this spice mix, follow the
same method as for the Nepali Barha
Masala (Nepali Garam Masala, see
page 190).

For best results, use this spice mix
within 2 weeks.

# Mangsahaar masala

*Meat garam masala*

### For the whole spices

1 tablespoon dried garlic flakes

5 dried red chillies, crushed

2 teaspoons cumin seeds

2 tablespoons coriander seeds

1 teaspoon timmur peppercorns,
   or Sichuan peppercorns

1 teaspoon cloves

2 teaspoons black peppercorns

4 black cardamoms

2 teaspoons green cardamoms

5 tejpaat (Nepali bay leaves), crushed

2 tablespoons jhhau (stone moss)

### For the ground spices

1 tablespoon freshly grated nutmeg
   (about ¾ of a whole nutmeg)

1 teaspoon hing (asafoetida)

*A screw-top jar or airtight container,
   for storing*

To make this spice mix, follow the
same method as for the Nepali Barha
Masala (Nepali Garam Masala, see
page 190).

For best results, use this spice mix
within 2 weeks.

# Sakahar barha masala

*Vegetable garam masala*

**For the whole spices**

1 tablespoon dried garlic flakes

5 dried red chillies, crushed

2 teaspoons cumin seeds

2 tablespoons coriander seeds

1 ¼ teaspoons black mustard seeds

1 teaspoon fenugreek seeds

1 teaspoon timmur peppercorns,
    or Sichuan peppercorns

2 teaspoons black peppercorns

4 black cardamoms

5 tejpaat (Nepali bay leaves), crushed

**For the ground spices**

1 tablespoon ground ginger

1 teaspoon turmeric

1 teaspoon hing (asafoetida)

~

To make this spice mix, follow the same method as for the Nepali Barha Masala (Nepali Garam Masala, see page 190).

For best results, use this spice mix within 2 weeks.

# Samagrah masala

*Whole spice garam masala*

Here all the spices are kept whole and activated in the hot oil at the beginning of the tempering technique, such as for the Karkalo Ko Pat Ko Tarkari (Colocasia Leaves Curry, see page 96).

2 teaspoons cumin seeds

2 tablespoons coriander seeds

1 teaspoon cloves

2 teaspoons black peppercorns

4 black cardamoms

2 teaspoons green cardamoms

5 tejpaat (Nepali bay leaves), crushed

7cm (2¾in) cinnamon stick,
    broken into shards

~

Simply mix all the spices and keep in a screw-top jar, or other airtight container. Use within 6 months.

# Sarso ledo

*Yellow mustard paste*

This paste is made with yellow mustard seeds, which are milder than brown or black mustard seeds. Soaking the seeds in vinegar will soften them for easier grinding. It will also reduce their bitterness.

This recipe makes a fairly generous quantity, but it will keep for up to 1 year, so store it in your refrigerator, ready to use when you need it.

300g (scant 1¾ cups) yellow mustard seeds

400ml (1⅔ cups) white wine vinegar

1½ teaspoons ground turmeric

1½ teaspoons caster (superfine) sugar

1½ teaspoons salt

*A large, sterilized screw-top jar*

Put the yellow mustard seeds in a non-metal container. Add the vinegar and soak the seeds overnight. They will absorb some of the vinegar. Drain and reserve the leftover vinegar.

Combine the drained seeds, turmeric, sugar and salt in an electric spice grinder or coffee grinder. Grind to a fine paste, adding some of the drained vinegar to loosen the paste. If you prefer less acidity, use water instead of vinegar at this stage.

Adjust the seasoning to taste, adding more, salt or sugar if needed.

Stored in a sterilized, large screw-top jar and refrigerated, this paste will keep for up to 1 year.

# Kurkure kamal kakdi, kurkure bhindi, kurkure pyaj

*Lotus root, okra and onion crisps*

The secret to making these vegetables extra crispy is to draw the moisture to the surface, then coat them with a mixture of cornflour (cornstarch), rice flour and gram flour just before frying.

I like to use the crisp lotus root to garnish the Swadilo Piro Tareko Valeko Masu (Crispy Chilli Chicken, see page 66), the okra for chutneys or snacking, and the onions for goat or chicken curries.

150g (5½oz) lotus roots, peeled and thinly sliced, or 150g (5½oz) fresh okras, tailed and each cut into 6–7 strips, or 150g (5½oz) red onions, cut into thin wedges

½ teaspoon salt

1 teaspoon Kashmiri chilli powder, or medium hot chilli powder

25g (¼ cup) cornflour (cornstarch)

25g (2½ tablespoons) rice flour

25g (2½ tablespoons) gram flour

1 litre (4 cups) vegetable oil, for deep-frying

1 teaspoon store-bought chat masala spice mix, to serve

*A kitchen thermometer*

Place the lotus roots slices (or okra strips, or red onion wedges) in a mixing bowl. Sprinkle with the salt and gently toss, making sure they are well coated and being careful not to break them. Sprinkle with the chilli powder and toss again, as before. Set aside for 10 minutes to let the moisture out (except for the onions).

Heat the oil in a deep-sided sauté pan until it reaches 140°C (250°F).

Meanwhile, in a separate bowl, whisk the 3 flours together. Add the seasoned lotus roots (or okra strips, or onion wedges). Toss gently until they are evenly coated with the flour mix. Separate the slices (or strips, or wedges) if they get stuck together. Transfer to a sieve (strainer) and shake to eliminate the excess flour.

Deep-fry in the hot oil in batches for 4–5 minutes, until golden, raising the temperature of the oil to 160°C (325°F) halfway through the cooking time. Drain on kitchen paper (paper towels) and sprinkle with chaat masala. The slices will crisp up as they cool down.

# Sweet Things & Drinks

In Nepal, we love sweet things! We eat them throughout the day for breakfast, as snacks and after meals. During festivals, an excessive amount of sweets are available from street stalls. Dipped in saffron syrup, with multiple shapes and textures, all the Nepali sweets are a feast for the eyes. The variety of sweets is again a reflection of our many communities.

Yogurt is an important part of the Newari diet. It is made from bhaisi (female buffalo) milk. Traditionally, we use clay pots to make yogurt. It is a perfect vessel to let the excess moisture evaporate, resulting in a thick and creamy yogurt. Thanks to the warm weather of the Terai, the milk quickly turns into yogurt overnight. Sikarni (Spiced Yogurt Dessert, see page 211) is a mixture of yogurt and cream which is left to ferment overnight. It is rich, slightly sour and delicately spiced. It was used to clear the palate during the extravagant feasts of the Rana dynasty (1846–1951) and is the perfect refreshing end to a spicy meal.

In the introduction to my recipe for Dahi Ra Maha (Honey Yogurt Drink, see page 206), I mention the famous Himalayan honey – a dark, thick nectar made by giant bees, which is harvested in the most dangerous conditions as the bees are experts at hiding their hives and often change location. It is sold at high prices to the Chinese, Japanese and Korean markets for its healing properties. The local Himalayan

communities who hunt for this honey consume it in low doses to boost the body's immune system. In high doses, it can be toxic, but Nepal also has a large variety of bees that produce delicious non-toxic honeys. Unfortunately, the production is barely enough for Nepal's own needs and very little is exported, though plans for developing Nepal's apiculture are ongoing.

We use a lot of gud (jaggery) in our cooking and in sweets. Sugar cane is pressed to release the sap and left to sit. Then the clear liquid at the top, without the sediments, is boiled until thick. The liquid gud is then moulded and left to cool down. It solidifies and is separated into blocks – the ones you buy in Asian food shops. It is high in minerals and an important remedy in Ayurvedic medicine. It helps warm the body in the winter, and is also considered as a detoxifier for the whole body and an immune system booster.

In this chapter, I have also included a dessert I tasted at one of the culinary school competitions in Kathmandu, at the Global Academy of Tourism and Hospitality Education. Every year, young, talented chefs graduate from the many culinary schools that are now operating in Kathmandu. I am proud to say that my own culinary journey has been an inspiration for these young chefs, and so I look to support their talent and aspirations in any way I can. I hope you enjoy the recipe for Lahre App (Himalayan Passion Fruit Cream, see page 112) as much as I do.

"Traditionally, we use clay pots to make yogurt. It is a perfect vessel to let the excess moisture evaporate, resulting in a thick and creamy yogurt. Thanks to the warm weather of the Terai, the milk quickly turns into yogurt overnight."

*Following pages:* Monks sit at the entrance to the Chiwong Monastery during the Sherpa festival of Mani Rimdu.

*Left:* Villagers grinding pulses (legumes) by hand in the Terai area of Nepal.

*Bottom left:* A women selling a colourful array of knitted woollen clothes, including hats and gloves, in Bhaktapur.

*Below:* A Buddhist prayer wheel.

# Dahi ra maha

*Honey yogurt drink*

Collecting honey has always been a dangerous job but nothing like the wild honey hunt on the steep cliffs of the Himalayas. The bees build their nests in the most inaccessible cliffs, away from predators. Once the nests are found, the honey hunters hang from precarious rope ladders, juggling two long poles – one to hold their collecting basket and the other to poke the nest and detach the nectar.

The Himalayan giant honey bees gather the pollen of nearby medicinal plants, making their honey not only praised for its exceptional rich flavour but also for treating infections. The springtime 'red honey' is believed to have hallucinogenic properties.

200g (scant 1 cup) natural (plain) Greek yogurt

45g (2 generous tablespoons) raw honey

60ml (¼ cup) whole (full-fat) milk, chilled

**To serve**

Rose syrup, for drizzling

Almond and pistachios kernels, finely shredded

Place the yogurt and honey in a mixing bowl. Whisk until well blended. Gradually whisk in the milk.

Spoon the mixture into four tall glasses, garnish with droplets of rose syrup and a sprinkle of chopped almonds and pistachios. Serve at once.

# Masala chiya

*Masala tea*

Everyone in Nepal has their own recipe for Masala tea. Mine includes lemongrass and tulsi. Also called holy basil, tulsi is an important herb both in religious rituals and for its medicinal properties (see page 17).

1 tablespoon strong black tea leaves

300ml (1 ¼ cups) whole (full-fat) milk

1 ½ tablespoons caster (superfine) sugar

2.5-cm (1-in) piece of cinnamon stick

2 green cardamoms, lightly crushed

15g (½oz) fresh ginger, peeled, sliced and lightly crushed

5-cm (2-in) piece of lemongrass (optional)

2 tulsi (holy basil) leaves (optional)

Bring 50ml (3 ½ tablespoons) of water to the boil in a small saucepan over medium heat. Reduce the heat to a simmer, add the tea leaves and leave to infuse for 1–2 minutes.

Add the milk and the rest of the ingredients, and simmer over low heat for a further 10 minutes.

Strain into a heatproof cup, discard the spices and serve at once, whilst hot.

# Sikarni

*Spiced yogurt dessert*

Sweet, lightly spiced and creamy, this dessert comes from the Newari cuisine of the Kathmandu valley where many households make yogurt every day. Thanks to the warm weather, the milk will turn into yogurt overnight. The origin of Sikarni is not clear, but it is thought to have been served as a refreshing end to the rich banquets prepared by the Royal Kitchen.

I use Greek yogurt in this recipe which is similar in consistency to Nepali yogurt. The preparation is placed in a muslin (cheesecloth) and hung overnight, allowing the soured cream to boost the fermentation process and the spices to infuse.

### For the hung yogurt

400g (1¾ cups) natural (plain) Greek yogurt

150g (⅔ cup) soured cream

75g (⅓ cup) double (heavy) cream

50g (¼ cup) caster (superfine) sugar

5 saffron threads, soaked in 1 teaspoon of warm water for 10 minutes

1 pinch of ground cinnamon

⅛ teaspoon freshly grated nutmeg

4 black peppercorns, finely crushed

### To finish

50g (½ cup) mixed dried fruits

Mix the yogurt, soured cream and double cream in a bowl until well combined.

Place a colander inside a separate bowl. Lay a large square of muslin (cheesecloth) inside the colander. Spoon the yogurt mixture into the muslin. Gather the side of the muslin to cover the yogurt. Place the whole thing in the refrigerator overnight. The whey will slowly drip into the bowl and after 12 hours, the yogurt mixture will be thicker.

The next day, transfer the yogurt mixture into a bowl. Add the sugar and spices and mix well. If the mixture is too thick, whisk in a little more cream or milk to loosen. Adjust the seasoning, adding more sugar or spices to taste.

Serve cold, topped with dried fruits.

# Lahre aap

*Himalayan passion fruit cream*

I was a judge for one of the food competitions at the Global Academy of Tourism and Hospitality Education in Kathmandu. I was so impressed by this passion fruit cream, with its perfect texture and flavour, that I asked Mr Khem Lakai, the principal, for the recipe. He was very happy to share it, just as I am happy to share it with you.

200ml (¾ cup) double (heavy) cream

50ml (3½ tablespoons) whole (full-fat) milk

Scraped seeds from ½ a vanilla pod (bean)

3 large egg yolks

40g (1½oz) caster (superfine) sugar

2 large passion fruit

*4 clay or ceramic ramekins, each 125-ml (½-cup) capacity*

*A roasting tin (pan) large enough to take the 4 ramekins*

Preheat the oven to 120°C (100°C fan/250°F/Gas ½).

Combine the cream, milk and vanilla seeds in a small saucepan. Heat over low heat until just below boiling point. Meanwhile, whisk the egg yolks and sugar in a large, heatproof bowl. Gradually pour the hot cream mixture onto the egg and sugar mixture, whisking constantly.

Halve 1 passion fruit and scrape the seeds and juice from one of the halves, (about 25 ml/1½ tablespoons) directly into the creamy mixture. Stir until well combined, then strain the cream mixture through a fine sieve (strainer) into a clean bowl.

Divide the cream mixture between the ramekins. Cover each one with foil. Place them in the roasting tin. Put the roasting tin on a shelf in the preheated oven, then very carefully pour sufficient boiling water into the tin to come halfway up the sides of the ramekins. (This water bath is known as a 'bain marie'.) Bake for 1 hour.

Combine the seeds and juice from the remaining 1½ passion fruit and set aside for serving.

Remove the roasting tin from the oven, then the ramekins from the bain marie. Leave to cool for 30 minutes. Chill in the refrigerator for 4–5 hours.

Serve chilled, topping each ramekin with a tablespoon of the reserved passion fruit pulp.

# Khajuria

*Fried cookies*

The delicious crumbly texture of these cookies comes from using ghee (clarified butter). Like many cookies in Nepal, they are eaten throughout the day, to accompany a cup of tea, or as an after-dinner treat.

The decorative parallel lines on one of their sides comes from a specially carved khajuria cookie press. To replicate this pattern, you can simply mark the lines on the dough with the prongs of a fork.

75g (generous ½ cup) roti (chapati) flour, or brown flour

125g (1 cup) plain (all-purpose) flour

60g (generous ¼ cup) caster (superfine) sugar

60g (4 tablespoons) ghee (clarified butter), melted

3 green cardamoms, seeds only

1 tablespoon raisins, chopped

1 tablespoon dried coconut flakes

About 60ml (¼ cup) whole (full-fat) milk

1 litre (4 cups) vegetable oil, for deep-frying

*A kitchen thermometer*

In a mixing bowl, combine both flours and the sugar, and whisk until well blended. Add the ghee and, using your fingers, rub the ghee into the mixture until it looks like fine breadcrumbs.

Mix in the cardamom seeds, raisins and coconut flakes.

Add the milk and mix with your hand until a firm dough forms. Cover the dough with a kitchen towel (dishcloth) and rest for 30 minutes, enough time to let the sugar melt into the dough.

Heat the oil in a deep-sided sauté pan until it reaches 160°C (325°F).

You can divide the dough into 15 small balls of 25g (1oz) each or, if you prefer, 10 larger balls of 35g (1¼oz) each. Roll each ball between the palms of your hands and flatten it into a thick patty. Using the prongs of a fork, mark parallel lines over the surface, only on one side. If you have a traditional Nepali cookie mould (see recipe introduction), press each patty into the grooves to mark the stripes.

Deep-fry the cookies, in batches, for 5–7 minutes. Remove them from the oil and drain on kitchen paper (paper towels). They will crisp up more as they cool. Once cool, serve with a fresh cup of Masala Chiya (Masala Tea, see page 209) or coffee.

These will keep, stored in an airtight container, for 1–2 weeks.

## About the author

Born and raised in the small village of Karjanha, in the province of Sagarmatha, South East Nepal, Santosh Shah developed a love for food from a very early age, thanks to his mother's cooking. Aged 14, Santosh left for India on a three-day train journey that would turn his life around. Starting out in the kitchens of an Indian hotel, he worked his way up the ranks in the world of hospitality and moved to the UK in 2010. Santosh has since worked with some of the best Michelin star chefs including Raymond Blanc, Atul Kochhar and Vivek Singh, and has held positions in London's top Indian restaurants from Dishoom to Cinnamon Kitchen and Benares. He won the hearts of the nation as a *MasterChef: The Professionals* finalist, wowing the judges with his passion for creating outstanding dishes inspired by the richness and diversity of Nepali cuisine.

## Acknowledgments

I am honoured to be bringing Nepali food to the world through this book and would like to thank everyone at DK who has worked with me to create it, including Stephanie Milner, Bess Daly, Kiron Gill, Louise Brigenshaw, Dave Brown, Julia Charles, Tony Phipps, Rebecca Parton, Sara Pinotti, Frances Gizauskas and the whole sales team.

A big thank you must also go to Valerie Berry who was a constant support to me while making this book – she is amazing! Our shoot team of Matt Russell, Tabitha Hawkins, Kitty Coles, Hannah Lemon and Valerie were fantastic, and I am very grateful for their creativity and for making everything look so incredible.

Thank you to Pandav Mahato, who inspired me to include the spice blends and thank you to Anju Basnet, who always helps me, for tasting the recipes and giving me advice about how to adapt my recipes for a home cook!

Thank you to Karna Sakya and Vivek Singh for reviewing the book and lending your kind words.

## Picture credits

The publisher would like to thank the following for their kind permission to reproduce their photographs:
*(Key: a-above; b-below/bottom; c-centre; f-far; l-left; r-right; t-top)*

**4 Unsplash:** Giuseppe Mondì. **10-11 Unsplash:** Azin Javadzadeh. **18-19 Shutterstock.com:** Tomasz Wozniak. **27 Alamy Stock Photo:** Ashley Whitworth (cla). **Getty Images / iStock:** Moonstone Images (br). **Shutterstock.com:** SeeVera (bl). **28-29 Shutterstock.com:** Piyawan Tantibankul. **49 Getty Images:** Feng Wei Photography. **50-51 Unsplash:** Avel Chuklanov. **75 Getty Images:** Feng Wei Photography (br); Nadeem Khawar (clb). **76-77 Getty Images / iStock:** Jedraszak. **89 Getty Images / iStock:** Bartosz Hadyniak (clb). **Robert Harding Picture Library:** Frank Bienewald (cla). **90-91 Shutterstock.com:** Aleksei Kazachok. **122 AWL Images:** Hemis (b). **123 AWL Images:** Hemis (b). **124 Getty Images iStock:** foto Voyager (b). **143 AWL Images:** Ian Trower (b). **144-145 AWL Images:** Hemis. **167 Shutterstock.com:** Aleksandar Todorovic. **168 Getty Images:** Boy_Anupong. **185 Alamy Stock Photo:** Frank Bienewald (cla). **Shutterstock.com:** Pavel Svoboda Photography (cl); Ashley Whitworth (br). **203 Alamy Stock Photo:** Benjamin Maclean (br). **AWL Images:** Hemis (cla); Ian Trower (bl). **204-205 AWL Images:** Hemis. **216-217 Getty Images:** girolame.

Publishing Director  Katie Cowan
Senior Acquisitions Editor  Stephanie Milner
Editors  Julia Charles, Kiron Gill
Development Editor and Food Stylist  Valerie Berry
Art Director  Maxine Pedliham
Managing Art Editor  Bess Daly
Project Designer  Louise Brigenshaw
Designer Dave Brown at APE Inc. Ltd

Jackets Coordinator  Jasmin Lennie
Senior Production Editor  Tony Phipps
Production Controller  Rebecca Parton
Photographer  Matt Russell
Prop Stylist  Tabitha Hawkins
Proofreader  Anne Sheasby
Indexer  Hilary Bird

First published in Great Britain in 2022 by
Dorling Kindersley Limited
DK, One Embassy Gardens, 8 Viaduct Gardens,
London, SW11 7BW

The authorised representative in the EEA is
Dorling Kindersley Verlag GmbH.
Arnulfstr. 124, 80636 Munich, Germany

Copyright © 2022 Dorling Kindersley Limited
A Penguin Random House Company
10 9 8 7 6 5 4 3 2 1
001–326712–Feb/2022

Text copyright © 2022 Santosh Shah
Santosh Shah has asserted his right to be identified as the author
of this work.

A CIP catalogue record for this book
is available from the British Library.
ISBN: 978-0-2415-3577-6

Printed and bound in Latvia

For the curious
**www.dk.com**